Spiritual Fitness

SPIRITUAL FITNESS

Everyday Exercises for Body and Soul

DORIS DONNELLY

HarperSanFrancisco
A Division of HarperCollins*Publishers*

Biblical quotations are from the New Revised Standard Version.

Chapter 2, "Praising," is an adaptation of "Impediments to Praise in the Worshipping Community," which appeared in *Worship* 66 (January 1992), 39–53.

Chapter 6, "Laughing," is an adaptation of "Divine Folly: Being Religious and the Exercise of Humor," which appeared in *Theology Today* 48 (January 1992), 385–398.

FIRST EDITION

Library of Congress Cataloging-in Publication Data
Donnelly, Doris.
    Spiritual fitness : everyday exercises for body and soul / Doris
Donnelly. — 1st ed.
        p. cm.
    Includes bibliographical references and index.
    ISBN 0–06–061899-X (alk. paper)
    1. Spiritual life—Christianity.   2. Spiritual exercises.
    3. Body, Human—Religious aspects—Christianity.   4. Man (Christian
theology) I. Title
    BV4501.2.D637   1993
    248.4—dc20   92-53923
                                                            CIP

93 94 95 96 97 ❖ HAD 10 9 8 7 6 5 4 3 2 1

To the women in my family
✦
My grandmothers,
Margaret Todzia Kowalczyk
and
Henrietta Dreyer Krimper
✦
My mother,
Betty Kowalczyk Krimper
✦
My daughter,
Margaret Hope Donnelly
✦
and
My daughter-in-law,
Christine Walsh Donnelly

*Therefore lift your drooping hands and strengthen your
weak knees, and make straight paths for your feet,
so that what is lame may not be put out of joint,
but rather be healed.*

Hebrews 12:12–13

CONTENTS

Foreword by Walter Brueggemann   *xi*

Acknowledging   *xiii*

Chapter 1   Listening   *1*

Chapter 2   Praising   *19*

Chapter 3   Eating   *41*

Chapter 4   Working   *65*

Chapter 5   Weeping   *91*

Chapter 6   Laughing   *111*

Chapter 7   Forgiving   *129*

Chapter 8   Persevering   *151*

Just Doing It   *169*

Index   *173*

FOREWORD

Doris Donnelly knows full well that being human is a wondrous gift from a generous God. But in this profoundly subversive book she speaks of the *task* of humanness that must be performed, a task requiring daily resolve, courageous investment of one's full self, and a willingness to grow into the gifts that constitute our God-given selves. She probes deeply the sorts of habits, gestures, and practices that make human wholeness possible, wholeness that must be worked intentionally against the antihuman values that dominate our society and its commodity commitments.

The author has thought long, noticed much, and prayed well about her proposals. Beyond that, she permits us inside her rich and resourceful scrapbook, testimony to those who have taken up this task of humanness. The book is loaded with references and hints across an amazing spectrum of saints, poets, writers, and unnoticed folk who have insisted upon wholeness for their life, and who have let us glimpse the risks and delights of their insistence. The book with its eight "exercises" is a powerful invitation to newness in faith.

As I read, I thought Doris Donnelly should have added a ninth exercise, namely, *reading*. That is, not reading just anything, but reading writing like that of Donnelly. But then, there isn't much written like Donnelly, so . . . read Donnelly. As I read, I sensed her largeness of spirit, gracefulness, and cunning good humor. I found the very reading itself an act of disclosure, mediation, and healing. Her book

matches well medium and message. The message is that human life
can be transformed. The medium is a daily act of the embrace of self
and the God who gives selves as gift. Donnelly not only shows us how
to embrace, but assists us in that work.

Walter Brueggemann
August 20, 1992
Decatur, Georgia

ACKNOWLEDGING

A writer needs food, warmth, encouragement, honesty, and friendship to bring a book to life.

I had it all.

My first debt is to Hugh T. Kerr, professor emeritus at Princeton Theological Seminary and longtime editor at *Theology Today*. It was he who thought the original idea proposed as an article should be book length and encouraged me to write. Tim Kerr died in March 1992, and this book stands as a modest tribute to his generosity and kindness.

Others provided support in many ways: Judith E. Smith, Carolyn North, and Jim Joy were always only a phone call away; Pam Tabar read the manuscript with a grammarian's care; Caron Napp, Nevin Mayer, and Mary Kay Sweeny at the John Carroll University Library were patient and prompt in handling many special requests; and Chip Freund was always available to provide computer information and assistance.

Kimberly Wood managed many details of this project as a graduate assistant. Mary Sharon Schumacher assisted in word processing the manuscript as she does everything else—with care and commitment. Regina Brett edited the final draft with skill and uncommon dedication; I am in her debt for accepting such a pressured task and accomplishing it so gracefully.

I am also grateful to Sally Wertheim, dean of the Graduate School at John Carroll University, whose enthusiasm bolstered me through a winter of disciplined writing. She has been an extraordinary mentor for me.

T George Harris connected with this project in its final stages and insisted, typically, that it not betray the human. I trust that the final manuscript shows that I took his advice to heart.

John Loudon, my editor at HarperSanFrancisco, listened, believed, and provided guidance wherever and whenever needed.

Other people have been integral to the creation of this book, whether they read the manuscript or not, and I want to thank Mary and Peter Funk, Mary Catherine Hunt, Joan Magnetti, Madonna Kling, John Mogabgab, Regina Bechtle, Ted Tracy, and especially Joseph Whelan.

Marilyn and Tim McCormick, my next-door neighbors, provided the presence in my life of their two beautiful baby daughters, Maureen and Claire, who put everything else into perspective.

My mom and dad, Betty and Theodore Krimper, as always provided support in every category, and the same is true of my children, Christopher and Peggy.

Doris Donnelly
July 31, 1992
Shaker Heights, Ohio

Chapter 1

LISTENING

If [you] will but listen intently to everyday sounds,
[you] will come to realization and at that instant
see the very Source.

PHILIP KAPLEAU, *THE THREE PILLARS OF ZEN*

Several years ago, I was interviewed for a job by a man who did nothing to hide the fact that he was a poor listener. He called me Dolores instead of Doris and then miscued on several other basic facts from my résumé. When he asked questions, my answers didn't seem to make any difference.

While he was talking nonstop, I recalled the story of the hostess of a cocktail party whose guests were so self-absorbed that when she passed the canapés and said, "Have one, darling, they're toasted arsenic," several guests absentmindedly thanked her and asked for the recipe.

At the end of my interview, I was offered the job. I suspected that my mental and even physical health would suffer from a nonlistening climate. So I declined.

Listening is so important that I urge you to commit yourself to it as the basic foundation for the other exercises in this book.

The fact is that everybody lives listening to something. But few live a life attuned at every level. Unless we do, however, we live less than a full life. We remain deaf in at least one ear.

By listening, I mean being open to other ideas and other opinions, even ones that you may not like, ones that are different from your own. I have not always found this easy. But it is crucial to listen patiently rather than jump to disagree: to listen rather than run, to hear first and respond later.

Also, as part of listening, I urge you to listen to yourself. Listen to your body. It speaks a language of its own, but one that you can understand if you try. Listen to your brain and your heart. All parts form a whole worth attending to.

To Listen Is to Heal

Several years after my interview, Dr. James Lynch verified my hunch about health and listening. Lynch, co-director of the Psychophysiological Clinic and Laboratories of the University of Maryland, discovered the therapeutic effects of listening. He studied a sample of hypertensive people who used words to keep others at a distance, who listened defensively, and who acted as though they were engaged in a fight rather than a dialogue. When the conversation would deteriorate into argument, Lynch would reveal some personal story of his own. When he did so, patients forgot themselves and listened, even if momentarily. In the process, their blood pressures fell to levels far lower than they had known in years.

Could it be, he wondered, that the experience of listening was responsible?

He invited a group of people to participate in an experiment to explore this hunch. For twenty minutes, participants were asked to relax and stare at a blank wall. For the next twenty minutes, they were asked to watch a tank of tropical fish. Monitored by a computer, the blood pressure of participants lowered more when they attended to the bubbling of the tank than to the blank wall. Lynch hypothesized that active listening was more therapeutic than passive relaxation.

He concluded that a genuine healing of the cardiovascular system takes place when we listen. According to his data, blood pressure rises when people speak and it lowers when people listen.

Instead of moving between listening and talking, the hypertensive was constantly on guard. As a result, blood pressure did not fall but instead rose higher the next time he or she spoke.

Lynch's results tell us some things about listening we may have suspected all along.

How Listening Differs From Hearing

Lynch's experiment suggests that the act of listening is not as passive as it first appears. To listen well involves heightened active skills that need to be practiced. His experiment also highlights the difference between hearing and listening. Therapist Robert Wicks writes that "hearing is an easy, passive process, [but] listening requires energy, motivation and patience." We are born with the gift of hearing, but listening is a gift that we need to nurture. Listen to the way parents relate to a four-week-old infant and to a four-year-old child to see the difference between hearing and listening. In the first instance, a father jingles his keys over a crib and is proud of his daughter as she turns toward the sound. She *hears*. A mother instructing her four-year-old son not to talk to strangers knows her son *hears*, but she wants more. She wants him to *listen*.

Hearing involves the proper functioning of auditory nerves. Listening assumes that more than sound is heard. Content must be absorbed.

The distinction between hearing and listening is critical for still another reason. Adults who only *hear* restrict their worlds and experience to what they already know. They hear what they want to hear. According to Joan Chittister: "Once I become my own message, there is nothing else to hear. No chance to change. Nothing but echoes of my own voice." We only expand and grow by taking in something new: that something new comes through listening.

Listening and Truth

Lynch offers another insight. There is a truth that opens up, a sense that emerges, and feelings that surface only with listening. You and I are much more inclined to disclose ourselves when someone is tuned in to us and our agenda. We are less likely to reveal ourselves in settings where know-it-all talking is going on.

Anne Morrow Lindbergh discovered the value and benefits of listening at the Maine seashore and wrote of her retreat in the now-legendary book *Gift from the Sea*. What drove Lindbergh to Maine was a messy and fragmented life without a core holding it all together. Wife of the celebrated hero Charles Lindbergh and mother of five children, she depicted the chaos in her life as spokes flailing about wildly without the hub of a wheel to center them. There is no English word for what she was living through, so she chose the German word *zerrissenheit*. Literally, it means "torn-to-piecehood," and its antidote is the inner, inviolable core, the single eye that effects balance, "no matter what centrifugal forces tend to pull us off center."

Lindbergh's centering happens when she listens to the seashells on her retreat and reflects on their messages for her:

> Solitude, says the moon shell. Every person, especially every woman, should be alone sometime during the year, some part of each week, and each day. How revolutionary that sounds and how impossible of attainment. To many women such a program seems quite out of reach.

To many men, also. But Lindbergh suggests that by really listening, we can create islands with calm centers in everyday life, and she argues that it is possible to give ourselves 5, 10, or 30 minutes of solitude with a walk, a run, a period of early morning or late night meditation.

Listening happens best if we do give ourselves time.

SILENCE SPEAKS

Silence is a necessary prerequisite whether we are listening to God, a friend, a relative, a lecture, or even to our pulse.

Inner silence is the most important kind, but inner silence usually flows from outer silence; both inner and outer silence offer a rhythm that slows things down on the outside so that the inside can come alive. Certain important discoveries are made only when there is silence. When the American novelist Tillie Olsen sought to describe the depth of women's experiences, she chose as her title *Silences,* for precisely that reason. The Danish author Isak Dinesen likewise reminds us that "where the story-teller is loyal, eternally and unswervingly loyal to the story . . . silence will speak." If Dinesen is correct, God's story can be heard again and again by each of us, but only if we are silent. Like Dinesen, T. S. Eliot writes of the nonnegotiable requirement of silence for discovering this way:

> *Where shall the word be found, where will the word*
> *Resound? Not here, there is not enough silence . . .*
> *The right time and the right place are not here*
> *No place of grace for those who avoid the face*
> *No time to rejoice for those who walk among noise*
>   *and deny the voice.*

Silence for Eliot and for us invites the word to be heard daily: the ordinary word or words, the word of God, and even Jesus who is *the* Word. Silence forms the "place of grace"; it shuns the noise that disables attentive listening and it welcomes the sometimes muffled, sometimes barely audible, and occasionally crystal clear voice of God.

The fluidity of silence gives us access to the depths of the psyche and to what the French symbolists term *l'état d'âme.* Silence is not a "tuning out" for passive receivers; it is rather a "tuning in," an opportunity to take notice and attend, gradually, to ourselves, to others, and to the Other. It is active, exhausting, and demanding in its concentration, yet at the same time, enabling and freeing. The peace at the heart of silence is always grace, and it prepares the ground, as no other resource does, for the path of dying to the self, a path that is the heart of the Christian paschal mystery, the dying and rising that is the Easter event of the faith.

The discovery of the self happens only in silence, because silence removes props and hiding places. "Speech," according to the British playwright Harold Pinter, "is a constant stratagem to cover nakedness." Silence enables the false self and the true self to struggle with no holds barred. Silence hunts us down until we come clean and discover who we are and who this God is who refuses to abandon us when we fail to love ourselves. Silence plunges us into a severe awareness of our naked selves.

ARE LISTENERS AN ENDANGERED SPECIES?

Anyone who listens well or is in the presence of another who is a good listener knows that listening takes practice and that very few people do it well.

Lee Iacocca, president of Chrysler Corporation, once praised the success of the Dale Carnegie program, which improved his public speaking ability. "I only wish," he wrote, "there were an effective program *for listeners.*" People think that successful salespeople are good talkers, but Iacocca believes success in sales is measured by how well a salesperson listens.

Frequently, communication problems are perceived as a need for improved verbal skills when what is really needed are better listening skills. The authors of *Egospeak* put it this way:

> We hear it said that conversation is a "lost art," as if all we need to do to regain it is to practice it, or to try to think more before we verbalize, or to study a dozen other rules preached in innumerable volumes. Quite the reverse is called for, yet is increasingly ignored—listening. Unless we listen to what the other person is saying, we cannot reply . . . effectively, nor can we take the next logical step in the conversation and permit it to flow freely and effortlessly.

On a daily basis, we all hear statements like these:

"But Dad, I told you this morning that I was going to be late. Weren't you listening?"

Or: "I asked for the report yesterday, the 14th. Don't you remember?"

Or: "I don't think you heard a word I said!"

The sorry fact that we are such poor listeners is only one part of the problem. The other sad truth is that when we need someone to listen to us—to share our grief or our joy or our puzzlement—the good listener is hard to find. Many people end up paying dearly and often for professional therapists and counselors when sometimes the attentive listening of a friend can suffice. The good listener turns out to be an endangered species.

GOOD LISTENERS

How can we tell the difference between the mediocre and the masterful, the indifferent and the insightful listener? What qualities distinguish good listeners from others?

Good listeners are patient.

The good listener does not rush us and is not frustrated when breakthroughs and solutions do not occur. The Apostle Paul singled out first of all, and presumably above all the other descriptions of love, that "love is patient" (1 Cor. 13:4). The good listener can possess many skills—can know how to look you in the eye, how not to fidget, and how to keep the conversation focused on your interests—but unless genuine patience marks the exchange, it is not quality listening.

Detroit inner-city pastor Father Edward Farrell illustrates the point about patience in a story about the death of a parishioner.

Lucy was a wise and deeply loved woman who had struggled against enormous odds to survive the complicated birth of a daughter a dozen years before. At that time, lying in a hospital bed with pain verging on delirium, Lucy heard medical staffers on the other side of the curtain predict that she would not last the night. But she pulled through, raised her daughter, and grew in that uncommon human awareness that distinguishes the very few. However, twelve years later, in a matter of months after cancer was diagnosed, Lucy was in the hospital again and near death.

When Father Farrell visited her, Lucy made a request that would define all future visits. "Don't say anything," Lucy asked. "And don't hurry." Lucy was asking for the presence of a human being who did not feel compelled to fill in the silences with words to make time pass. She wanted the company of a friend who would not evade being human by reciting stereotyped platitudes about God's will and heavenly peace. She needed someone to be in touch with the pain and sadness she knew as a single parent leaving behind a teenage daughter, as well as the hope, in spite of the odds, that somehow she would survive. Lucy was looking for a contemplative listener, someone not on a schedule, someone willing and astute enough to embrace silence. Such a person would listen to the verbal and nonverbal signals of the heart.

Lucy found that person in her pastor. But she gave him something, too. She left him (and us) the formula for the good listener: "Don't say anything. And don't hurry."

The composer and musician Paul Williams wrote in the liner notes of one of his records: "There are those who listen and those who wait to talk. This album is dedicated to the listeners."

Lucy and Paul Williams were looking for the same thing that we are.

Good listeners are alert.

The Gospel of John tells a story about Jesus in casual conversation with a Samaritan woman. The exchange between them begins about water and develops into intimate revelations concerning the woman's life and the identity of Jesus (see John 4:7–42).

What made this Samaritan woman different from the chummy little group of men traveling with Jesus was that she was a good listener. She was up front, attentive, and responsive. Jesus may have been delighted to meet her since he spent so much of his time among people who missed the point of what he was saying.

This woman was a good listener because she assumed that she could learn something. She paid attention and asked questions. She was willing to be surprised. She immediately noticed that a Jewish man broke protocol by asking her, a Samaritan woman, for a drink of water. She knew that Jews and Samaritans did not share the same cups or bowls, so she raised his behavior as an issue.

Jesus responded just as frankly: "If you knew . . . who it is that is saying to you, 'Give me a drink,' you would have asked him, and he would have given you living water" (John 4:10).

She could have scratched her head and walked away, but something in Jesus prompted her to probe his response. In doing so, she learned she was in the company of an extraordinary person who claimed to be the Messiah. There was no reason for her to doubt that claim, especially since he told her, without condemning her, of sins she thought were secretly tucked away.

Good listeners have the ability to invite disclosure. When we are in the presence of someone who listens well we find ourselves saying more than we expected to say. That happens when someone asks just the right question or provides a climate of trust in which we feel comfortable to be ourselves. In such situations, we say things like, "I didn't plan to get into all of this," or "I didn't plan to talk so much."

Jesus provided that climate for the woman at the well. But the woman also provided the opportunity for Jesus to talk about himself and to reveal who he was and what he was about. She drew him out. He drew her out. They listened to each other.

Good listeners do not run away when they hear something they do not want to hear.

The Samaritan woman was vulnerable; she left herself wide open to what Jesus said and it changed her life. When Jesus exposed her promiscuity—the five men in her life—she did not deny it or make excuses. She acknowledged the emptiness in her life and asked for the water that he promised would satisfy her forever.

How odd that someone outside the inner circle of followers—and a woman at that!—should be the first one to catch on to the magnanimous promises of Jesus and preach them to others. It happened partially because she listened so carefully, allowing God's word to take on a life of its own. The inner urgency of the message of Jesus inspired her to act.

Listeners often hear something for which they are unprepared, and even things they would rather not hear. There is a vulnerability associated with listening, a sphere we enter where, as open listeners, we may meet the unexpected or the unwanted. The process of listening is not always in our control, and what we hear may shake us up or wake us up. Good listening is a way of learning about ourselves and growing into a new awareness.

To be a vulnerable listener is to be open to being wounded. It is the occupational hazard of listening well.

Our pride is wounded when we don't have the answer to another's problem. Or when our "answer" is rejected. Being vulnerable means being present to someone else and forgetting our own agenda. Listening means just that—listening. Not assuring. Not solving. Not answering. Just listening.

The listening we do, or that someone does for us, has a power of its own. At the very least, it does not pull us away from other human beings but instead makes a community of care possible.

Good listeners are faithful.

We always resent advice givers when we are looking for listeners. Advice givers consider it their proper role to reprimand and take charge of our lives. They are often intrusive, sometimes painfully so, and they tend to be faithful to their advice, not to us.

Faithful listeners are different. Faithful listeners are not interested in bossing us around or scolding us. Nor do we sense indifference, disbelief, or disapproval from them. Faithful listeners recognize the jam we are in and offer quiet assistance, or vocal advocacy on our terms, not theirs.

Good listeners are people who accept us in our troubles without insisting that *they* told us so and that this is how *they* forecasted our future would unravel if we did not listen to *their* earlier pearls of advice. They take us beyond human listening with their fidelity and attention. They give us a glimpse of how God listens.

LET THE SPEAKER BECOME A LISTENER

We all have heard about the faithful God, the accepting God, and the compassionate God. One cannot read the Hebrew Scriptures or the New Testament without concluding that God is also a very good listener. No prerequisites seem to have been needed for talking to God. God was always approachable.

People in the Old Testament were not reluctant to come before Yahweh in anger, fear, or anxiety. Job, a faithful follower, angrily demanded an explanation from Yahweh for his afflictions: "How many are my iniquities and my sins? Make me know my transgression and my sin. Why do you hide your face, and count me as your enemy?" (Job 13:23–24). Cain approached God in fear after he murdered his brother Abel. And the widow Naomi's distress was palpable as she grieved the loss of her two sons, convinced that the hand of the Lord had turned against her (see Ruth 1:13).

The prevailing assumption was that Yahweh was there, able and eager to help, and that Yahweh would listen to the human voice in supplication. "Incline your ear," the Psalmist petitioned (Ps. 17:6). Yahweh inclined an ear consistently.

And something changed as a result. In the process of venting steam or joy, or despair or hope, what changed was not Yahweh but the ventilator. The change happened when the speaker became listener and heard, maybe for the first time, the living, loving, accepting, unthreatening, but bold and searing word of God.

The lesson about listening is nowhere better taught than in the story of Elijah and his quest for God. No one can fault Elijah for looking for God in razzle-dazzle thunder and pyrotechnical displays. Where else would God be? But when Elijah looked there, God was missing. And when Elijah tried to shake out God from the powerful wind, God was not there either. Only when Elijah became a listener attentive enough to hear "a sound of sheer silence" (1 Kings 19:12) did he find God.

All the extraneous equipment in the world does not matter; in fact, it can get in the way of our hearing if it encourages us to concentrate on technique and not on the source.

Elijah stands as someone who learned not only that God is faithful, but also that God is faithful on God's own terms. When God responds by listening faithfully, God responds with words we *need* to hear more than with those we *want* to hear.

JESUS LISTENED TO MORE THAN WORDS

In the New Testament, Jesus, in the tradition of the priests, prophets, and kings of the Old Testament, listened to the people. Someone who once recorded the New Testament on tape discovered that Jesus's actual words took up only eleven minutes out of a total of several hours of the Gospels. Jesus, in other words, spent more time listening than he did speaking.

The pattern for Jesus as Listener involved absorbing the total scene. He listened with his whole being. He was particularly attuned to body language: one woman who had hemorrhaged for twelve years maneuvered through a crowd and, hoping to be cured, touched the tassel of his cloak (Luke 8:44). She never spoke a word, but Jesus knew her request without hearing her verbalize it.

Jesus also listened to gestures. Another woman interrupted a dinner party at Simon the Pharisee's house, washed Jesus's feet with her tears, and dried them with her hair (Luke 7:36–49). Jesus read what she did as a sign of love and repentance that transcended the ordinary. He listened to hearts and to silence. He also knew how to read silence as guilt or awe. And he read faces with uncanny precision, separating the phony from the friend with stunning accuracy.

Jesus recognized that his disciples were deficient at listening, so he urged them often to "hear." The danger of hardened hearts not open to the word was real and it compromised their mission. "Let anyone with ears to hear listen! . . . Pay attention to what you hear; the measure you give will be the measure you get, and still more will be given to you." (Mark 4:23–24).

Jesus often used parables to jolt people into listening. With an inexhaustible supply of stories to tell, Jesus knew how to turn the tables on those who gathered to hear them. But these were not stories about "other people" even though they may have sounded that way. These were stories about the listeners themselves, their lives, their choices, and God's presence among them. What people listened to, then, was not simply a story about a frazzled woman who lost some money and spent hours looking for it (Luke 15). They also heard a story about a God who is unrelenting in the search for any one of us if we become lost.

It was not always comfortable for those in the crowd listening to Jesus. To hear about someone else's problems is one thing, but to hear about failings and self-deceptions of one's own is entirely different.

The challenge of listening to the parables remains the same for us. When we hear stories of shrewd business people, unscrupulous employees, runaway children, and unfaithful spouses, how is it possible to miss the point that in our time children are still troubled, families still in crisis, and business ethics still in disarray? If we really listened, how could we not do something to change the status quo?

People who listen to God in prayer put the world on alert that they are trying to hear more clearly the voice of God and that both they and the world may change when they do. "When we start listening to the Word of God, to others around us, to those with wise hearts and tried souls," writes Joan Chittister, "life changes from the dry and independent to the compassionate and meaningful."

BENEFITS OF LISTENING

What are the benefits of listening?

To listen well is to tap into the contemplative side of ourselves. We not only wind up listening to people more effectively but also become more aware of the world around us. e. e. cummings is one of many poets who understands the transformation effected by contemplative listening:

> i thank you God for this most amazing day:
> for the leaping greenly spirits of trees
> and a blue dream of sky: and for everything
> which is natural which is infinite which is yes
> . . .
> (now the ears of my ears awake and
> now the eyes of my eyes are opened)

Good listening not only opens ears; it opens eyes, too.

To listen is to widen the horizons of our relationships.

Opening ourselves to others is another way of extending our range of human experience. Caring at the deep level entailed in listening makes friendship possible. A friend is one who listens.

To listen is to make life multidimensional. One-dimensional living is what ego-centered people settle for. There is no effective, life-giving listening within such people. They spend all of their time talking nonstop about themselves. These persons can't wait to chime into your story with their story. "How was your vacation?" turns into an opportunity to tell you how their vacations were . . . for the last thirty years.

To listen is to become healthier. Listening has many therapeutic benefits for us, not the least of which is improved cardiovascular fitness. Listening quiets us down and puts us in a frame of mind that lessens anxiety and stress.

TO EXERCISE LISTENING

These exercises have been most helpful to me:

1. *Take time each evening to review the day aware of conversations.* Did you talk too much? Was somebody else trying to say something that you blocked, unintentionally or deliberately, or were too preoccupied to hear?

There are usually plenty of opportunities to correct such situations. The direct and honest approach is by far the most effective: "I thought of you and our conversation last night and began to wonder what you meant when you said you were considering changing jobs," or "It took me a while to react to the news about your mother's illness . . . I just want you to know that I'd like you to call on me if I can be of any help at all."

2. *Be aware that people speak with more than words and listen with more than ears.* Slowly and unself-consciously become aware of body language: eye contact, posture, clothing, grooming. Someone may be sending you messages before a word is spoken.

3. *Listen for feelings, not just for facts.* If a friend undergoes a mastectomy, or a neighbor becomes a father for the first time, *listen,* and do not assume you know the feelings (or the facts, for that matter). Surface behavior and communication style (anger, impatience, coldness) can mask the real message (of fear, insecurity, need for warmth or assurance).

4. *Be available as a listener to others.* In this exercise, charity begins at home. Listen to those closest to you.

5. *Resist the urge to offer advice.* A teenage daughter who has just failed her driver's exam does not want to hear advice on how to pass the next test. At least, not right away. Most likely, you're being called on to be a vulnerable, patient listener when she tells you the story.

6. *Share of yourself when appropriate.* When members of Alcoholics Anonymous and Weight Watchers listen to the stories of others, they provide empathic backup; their aim is togetherness rather than one-upmanship.

7. *Honor the confidentiality of what you've been told.* That means no leaks, no hints, and no telling the story with fictitious names. Curious people who have no right to information are able to put two and two together and figure out real names behind camouflaged tales. Betraying someone else's deepest expression of intimacy will also keep you away from your own.

8. *Listen to your body.* Is your body telling you things you don't want to hear? Is it saying "Slow down" or "Move faster" or "You are ugly"? Is your body in pain? The ordained minister and therapist Flora Slosson Wuellner comments that "we spend a lifetime centered around the necessities of feeding, clothing and sheltering our bodies, and we anxiously or impatiently take them to doctors when we are sick. But we almost never think about them in depth or listen to their signals of stress and distress."

9. *Learn to "listen between the lines."* Pay attention to your own pattern of disclosure. Note how you use pauses and clue words to invite the listener to greater intimacy.

10. *Tell the good listeners in your life how grateful you are for their patient attentiveness.* Acknowledge it for what it is—a rare gift.

11. *Practice being comfortable with silence.* Don't fill in the void with words. Practice not speaking and not getting uptight over pauses. Respect the fact that another listener, God, is present in the conversation, and perhaps that inaudible listener is now speaking to the heart of the one you are listening to. Ask yourself whether you would want to interrupt that conversation.

God speaks through ordinary events and ordinary people. God speaks on God's terms, in unexpected ways, and through the least likely of ordinary events and ordinary people.

We need to still the heart and wait and trust that God will speak.

NOTES

The epigraph comes from *The Three Pillars of Zen* by Roshi Philip Kapleau (New York: Doubleday Anchor Books, 1989), 316.

James J. Lynch describes his work on listening in his book *The Language of the Heart: The Human Body in Dialogue* (New York: Basic Books, 1985).

Robert Wicks's remarks concerning the nonpassiviity of listening come from his book *Helping Others* (New York: Gardner Press, 1982), 6, 10.

Joan Chittister, O.S.B., *Wisdom Distilled from the Daily* (San Francisco: Harper San Francisco, 1991), 24, is the source for the insight about listening and becoming our own message.

Anne Morrow Lindbergh's retreat in Maine is recounted in *Gift from the Sea* (New York: Pantheon Books, 1975). The *zerrissenheit* story is found on 29 and 56; the moon shell reflection on 48.

See Tillie Olsen's book *Silences* (New York: Delacorte Press/Seymour Lawrence, 1978).

The remarks from Isak Dinesen are from "The Blank Page," in *Last Tales* (Chicago: University of Chicago Press, 1967), 100. She comments further: "Who then tells a finer tale than any of us? Silence does."

T.S. Eliot's words are from "Ash Wednesday," in *The Complete Poems and Plays* (New York: Harcourt, Brace & Co., 1952), 65.

Harold Pinter's remarks come from "Between the Lines," a speech to the Seventh National Student Drama Festival in Bristol, recorded in the *Sunday Times* (London), March 4, 1962, 25.

See Lee Iacocca with William Novak, *Iacocca: An Autobiography* (New York: Bantam, 1984), 58, for the comment about listening.

The authors, Edmond G. Addeo and Robert E. Burger, are quoted from their book, *Ego Speak* (Radnor, PA: Chilton Book Co., 1973), xiii.

The name of Edward Farrell's parishioner was changed for reasons of privacy.

The Paul Williams quotation comes from the book by Robert Wicks, cited earlier, 13.

A superb essay on listening and the other who listens is Douglas Steere's "On Listening to Another," in *The Doubleday Devotional Classics*, Vol. III, edited E. by Glenn Hinson (Garden City, NY: Doubleday, 1978), 205–257.

Joan Chittister's book has been cited earlier. The quote about life changing as we listen to the Word of God comes from page 20.

e. e. cummings, *Poems 1923–1954* (New York: Harcourt, Brace & Co., 1954), 464, is the source for "i thank you God."

Flora Slosson Wuellner's comments on listening to the body can be found in her article "Prayer and Our Bodies," *Weavings 2* (November–December 1987), 14.

Chapter 2

PRAISING

But more than anything else,
God love admiration.
ALICE WALKER, *THE COLOR PURPLE*

I was at a girls' Little League baseball game recently when an eight year old whacked a ball clear out of the grass lot. Several (most!) of the parents *whose children were on the same team* barely acknowledged the event. Many adults turned and looked the other way when the girl came into the stands at the end of the game to be hugged by her parents. Did some parents feel their own daughters' accomplishments would be lessened if they praised the home-run "queen for a day"? Maybe so. Yet the inability of the group to share the happiness of the event left everyone diminished.

In their best-selling book *The One-Minute Manager,* Ken Blanchard and Spencer Johnson urge us to catch people "doing something right" and offer one minute's worth of praise right there on the spot. Their strategy is part of a larger plan to create a climate where people feel good about themselves, because only people who have a sense of self-worth are able to achieve their full potential.

What some of their clients learn about themselves when they try to put this formula into practice is that one minute of praise is surprisingly difficult. What more is there to say beyond "Good job!" or

"Great hit!" which accounts for only two of sixty seconds? People soon learn that they are inept at praise. They learn that they are far better at criticizing than they are at affirming. In fact, one minute of criticism seems like only a beginning, while one minute of praise often seems like an eternity.

We need praise. We need to give it as a proper response to people, to God, and to events as they unfold around us. To be tightfisted about praise is to be half alive, with eyes squinting, with heart and mind fiercely determined to shun beauty. But we need to be on the receiving end of praise, too, because without it we wither and die.

The ability to affirm others is one of the keys to joy. The word *affirm* derives from a Latin root that means "to build up." We build up when we affirm others, are built up when someone affirms us. C. S. Lewis called praise "inner health made audible." The exercise of giving praise will open up a contemplative side of your life and draw you into new dimensions of awareness and vitality.

"WE CANNOT BE CONTENT UNLESS WE PRAISE YOU"

Our embarrassment and ineptitude with praise, as identified by Blanchard and Johnson, raise some important questions. Why are so many of us misers when it comes to affirming others? Why is the simple act of praise so difficult for so many?

Christians and Jews may sense a certain irony connected with these questions about praise. After all, people from the Judeo-Christian tradition know, if not by instinct then certainly through their spiritual formation, that praise lies at the heart of who they are. To be nonpraisers contradicts their identity. Being Jewish or Christian has to do with giving God glory. The Psalms say so over and over again. "Praise the Lord, all you nations! Extol him, all you peoples!" (Ps. 117:1). "Sing praises to the Lord with the lyre, with the lyre and the sound of melody" (Ps. 98:5).

The Psalms are the basic but incomparable source book for all we need to know about praise. Not only is God worthy of praise, but also the ability to praise is a sign that we are fully alive, responding spontaneously and fully to someone or something we cherish. "There cannot be such a thing as true life without praise," the biblical scholar Claus Westermann wrote. "Praising and no longer praising are related to each other as are living and no longer living." The Psalmist put it this way: "Let me live, that I may praise you" (Ps. 119:175). Centuries ago, St. Augustine reminded us that we are born to praise and that we live incompletely and unhappily unless we are about the work of praising God. "The thought of You," Augustine wrote, "stirs us so deeply that we cannot be content unless we praise You, because You made us for yourself and our hearts are restless until they rest in You."

The New Testament reinforces the insights of the Old. Jesus was an effective and frequent praiser. Once, to the chagrin of his followers, he praised the faith of an enemy soldier who was convinced that Jesus had the power to cure his servant. The soldier insisted that a visit to the servant's bedside was unnecessary, certain that Jesus could effect the cure from afar. Jesus, "amazed at him," observed that such faith was rare indeed (see Luke 7:1–10).

Mary, the mother of Jesus, is another biblical model of one who praises. She praised God when she accepted the news that she was to give birth to the Messiah: "Surely, from now on all generations will call me blessed . . . for the Mighty One has done great things for me" (Luke 1:48–49). Following in the footsteps of Mary, saints of all ages have been people of praise. St. Francis of Assisi is generally regarded as the unofficial apostle of praisers. His Canticle of Brother Sun remains a masterpiece of affective, spontaneous, genuine praise: "All praise be yours, through Sister Moon and Stars, through Brother Wind and Air, through Sister Water, through Brother Fire, through Sister Earth, our mother, who feeds us in her sovereignty."

PRAISE IS TELLING THE TRUTH

In a sense, praise is nothing more than telling the truth, but like the truth, it is often in short supply. "Praise, like gold and diamonds, owes its value only to its scarcity," the essayist Samuel Johnson wrote in 1791.

Not much has changed since then.

As rare as praise is, opportunities and reasons for it abound. All we need do is recognize the detail of someone or something—a flawless jump shot, a Bach concerto, Boston at sunset—and allow ourselves to be "taken in," absorbed, intoxicated. Praise is often as simple as that: an unself-conscious choice that brings its own gentle side effects.

Praise begins by letting the other just "be." That kind of being presupposes the ability to forget oneself. It belongs to perceptive, open, and truthful people capable of admiring and adoring others.

People who are closed, bitter, self-preoccupied, and in need of ego strokes will never be able to praise. Failure to praise often says less about the object of praise and more about the people who choose not to do it. The words of C. S. Lewis are pertinent:

> The humblest, and at the same time, most balanced and capacious minds, praised most, while the cranks, misfits and malcontents praised least. The good critics found something to praise in many imperfect works; the bad ones continually narrowed the list of books we might be allowed to read. The healthy and unaffected [person], even if luxuriously brought up and widely experienced in good cookery, could praise a very modest meal; the dyspeptic and the snob found fault with all.

Our ease at praising determines the company we keep and who keeps company with us.

PRAYER AND PRAISE

Some say that prayers of praise are the hardest. The eminent theologian Karl Barth wrote that the "praise of God is the most endangered and the most dangerous undertaking of the Church."

There are thousands of reasons to praise God daily. All we have to do is open our eyes and notice any one of the ways that God draws us, speaks to us, and loves us to find cause for praise. When we do not praise, it does not mean that God is absent from our lives, but that our eyes are not open wide enough. Because we frequently take God for granted, we may need to cultivate a sense of awareness of God's presence in our lives and grow in an appreciation of where God is and what God is doing. When we begin to notice, we can do nothing but sigh and praise, like the author of the Psalms, who seemed to know from experience that God is active, personal, and present in our lives. "Come and see what God has done: [God] is awesome" (Ps. 66:5). "Let everything that breathes praise the Lord" (Ps. 150:6).

Praise can take a variety of forms, from singing to silence. Sometimes our praise needs to be shouted from the housetops; sometimes, whispered in tears. Praise unleashes our joy and lets it have full sway over us. When we praise, we are not just experiencing joy, we are extending joy to others. C. S. Lewis wrote: "I think we delight to praise what we enjoy because the praise not merely expresses but completes the enjoyment; it is its appointed consummation."

Praise is possible only when someone or something exceeds our expectations. Even when we set our sights very, very high, some unexpected experience pulls the rug from under us. A spectacular vista beckons, or we hear Dame Kiri Te Kanawa at the Met, or we watch Stefi Graf at Wimbledon, and our expectations, as high as they are, are eclipsed. When we least expect it, we are caught off guard, and praise spontaneously erupts in response to what we have witnessed, depending only on how open-eyed and open-hearted we are. For the person of faith, a sustained double vision directs the praise: one values the gift *and* the giver because one sees God in it and it in God. Only at that point do we understand the secret at the heart of praise: what brings fulfillment is rejoicing in what God has done for us—not in what we do for God.

GOD SPRINGS SURPRISES
WHEN WE LEAST EXPECT THEM

Perhaps no one more clearly makes the point about how God springs surprises than the American novelist Alice Walker in *The Color Purple*. At one point, Celie and Shug are in earnest conversation about God when Shug corrects Celie's vision of how God manages the universe. Life is not, as Celie thinks, a matter of scurrying about doing good deeds to earn God's approval. It is, rather, taking time to notice, appreciate, and praise what God has provided for *our* pleasure and enjoyment. "I think it pisses God off if you walk by the color purple in a field somewhere and don't notice it," Shug counsels.

The simple insight is that God created the world for our delight, and we bring that delight to completion when we notice and praise God's handiwork. "People think pleasing God is all God care about," Shug tells Celie. "But any fool living in the world can see it always trying to please us back. . . . It always making little surprises and springing them on us when we least expect." The insight baffles Celie, and if we are honest about this, it baffles us, too. We spend too much energy trying to become acceptable to God and in the process miss the minute-by-minute unfolding of God's creation. Celie gives eloquent voice to the puzzlement:

> Well, us talk and talk bout God, but I'm still adrift.
> . . . I never notice nothing God make. Not a blade of
> corn (how it do that?) not the color purple (where it
> come from?). Not the little wildflowers. Nothing.

Celie's reflection leads to a transformation: she becomes a praiser. The invitation to praise is open to us, too. All that is required is to relax, behold, and speak the truth about a God who was thoughtful enough to make the color purple.

PRAISING AND THANKING

Giving thanks and giving praise are two different things; one can exist without the other. We can, for example, *praise* a child for learning the alphabet, but we *thank* the cashier for making change. Praise is not the same as thanks, nor is praise equal to "extra" thanks, because the focus of thanking is always on the one doing the thanking, not on the one receiving it. We say: "Thank you for feeding *me*." "Thank you for driving *me*." "Thank you for caring for *my* mother."

But praise zeroes in on the one being praised, and it sounds like this: "*You* are wonderful!" "How terrific *you* are!" In and of yourself, without any reference to me or anyone else, I see in *you* something worthy to be praised. Sometimes, we praise some "thing" a person did or has, but once again we move ourselves out of the picture: "Your house is beautiful!" "You dance so gracefully!" Notice that the "for me" tagline is missing when we praise. One who thanks might say, "Thanks for picking up my car for me." Of the same episode, the praiser might say, "You are so generous. I can't believe what a thoughtful friend you are!" The focus shifts away from the self to the other in praise.

If the line between thanks and praise is a thin one, this is not a new discovery. The respected biblical scholar Claus Westermann explains that as far back as the writing of the Hebrew Scriptures, our word *thank* had no corresponding equivalent in the Psalms, and that the Hebrew word often translated as *thank* most often meant "praise." For the Hebrew, then, thanks and praise were often the same, justifying why we connect the two.

Yet Westermann summarizes the difference between our modern use of thanks and praise this way:

+ In praise, the one being praised is elevated (magnified); in thanks, the one thanked remains in his or her place.

+ In praise, I am directed wholly toward the one being praised and away from myself; in thanks, "I" become part of the thank you, for it is *my* thanks.

+ Praise has a public dimension—I want others to know where my praise is directed and/or to participate with me. Giving thanks, on the other hand, is private, for it need concern no one except the one thanking and the one being thanked.

+ Praise is essentially joyful, but giving thanks can be obligatory and sometimes has the character of being required. Praise can never be forced, but thanks must often be.

The grandest praise is given to God, but praise also needs to be lavished on our families, on our children, parents, and spouses, as well as on friends, neighbors, employers, employees, and co-workers. We need to think about the consequences of too little praise and the poverty that is ours when we fail to do our share of praising. We need to tap the power and energy that is ours in the Spirit in every act of praise.

OBSTACLES TO PRAISING

If praise is so desirable and so attractive, and if our need for it is so constant, why is so little given? The obstacles to praise can be explained in several ways.

In the first place, people don't praise because they don't know how to do it. This certainly sounds strange. Does someone exist who doesn't know *how* to praise?

Many relationships disintegrate because of the inability of one partner to nourish the other with praise. Marriages collapse when wives feel that husbands do not appreciate them by saying "thanks" every once in a while, let alone by praise. Fathers complain that no one values all they do for their families. And many employees work devotedly for years without praise from the boss, receiving only a formal "thanks" at their retirement dinners. The absence of praise sometimes prompts people to work even harder and longer to force superiors to notice them and their efforts, but all of this is done in a spirit of duty, not freedom, and the stress connected with the effort induces a weariness that often ends in burnout.

Yes, it sometimes happens that people do not know how to praise. Instead, they may tease, cajole, or mock. Instead of praising a child's efforts, they may make comments like "You were good, but you weren't as good as your brother" or "You made it, but you almost missed." Or faint praise is followed by "but" and a comment that demolishes the achievement (and often the person as well). In practice (and nonpraisers seem to practice a great deal), it sounds something like this: "That wasn't bad, but you'll have to try a lot harder to have a really strong backhand."

Not knowing how to praise takes many forms, one of which is sheer awkwardness: "I've been meaning to talk to you about your work as a volunteer. I mean, what I want to say is, your work, well your work . . . How do you think your work went? I mean, because I thought it was fine. Even really good."

Or we may have been raised in families or been part of institutions where our adult role models were good at criticizing but not at praising. One report about lack of praise in the school setting is especially disturbing:

> Eighty percent of students entering school feel good about themselves and who they are. By the fifth grade only 20 percent have high self-esteem. By the time students become seniors in high school, the percentage who have managed to keep a positive level of self-esteem has dropped to 5 percent.
>
> Students encounter the equivalent of 60 days a year of reprimanding, nagging and punishment. During 12 years of schooling a student is subject to 15,000 negative statements. That's three times the amount of positive statements received.

How does *anyone* grow up to be an affirming adult?

This statistic also highlights the very real possibility that some people have never been praised. What then?

When praise doesn't happen at all, the nonaffirmed person feels a void so vast and a hunger so profound that until it is satisfied, he or she is incapable of reaching out and affirming others. The need for affirmation is often so deep that no matter what worthy occasion or worthy person comes into view, a paralysis renders us impotent to praise. The tragedy is that without the experience of being affirmed and affirming another, our spiritual muscles are so flabby that we have no strength to praise anyone else, including God.

Second, people do not praise because they do not want to do it. When it comes right down to it, this is why most praising does not get done. It is usually not a question of knowing how to praise or discerning the appropriate target of praise. Most likely, *we decide not to praise*.

The various reasons for not wanting to praise fall under three main categories: the social stigma attached to praising, competition, and jealousy.

Sometimes, people choose not to praise because praise is considered soft and indulgent. To live without praise is considered the test of a real man or a successful woman. The late football coach Vince Lombardi prided himself on rarely praising any of his players or coaching team, even though the Green Bay Packers won the Super Bowl twice. For Lombardi, the absence of praise toughened his team and helped them win. He thought that to praise them would have created a dependency on praise, and the "macho" world of pro football thrives without that fluff. Lombardi wasn't alone. There are teachers, grandparents, administrators, bosses, pastors, executives, parents, and other adults who would agree with Lombardi's principle: to withhold praise is character building.

Closely connected with this axiom is the belief that needing praise is a weakness. A hardworking lawyer I know tells this story: "I worked through the night preparing briefs, making calls, researching precedents. I knew (and so did my client) that the cards were stacked against us, so I worked weekends, holidays, and I temporarily surrendered my personal life and interests to see him through a very tough time.

"On the day of our first court victory, my client ran out of the courthouse and went home without so much as a handshake for me. I told him later how disappointed I was that he never even said thanks."

The client was genuinely surprised. "You mean," he said, "after being a lawyer all these years, you still need to be stroked?"

Echoing in the back of my mind are the voices of children asking the same of their parents. "Dad, you always do a great job. You don't need us to tell you that, do you?" There are the voices of employees and employers; of ministers and congregations, too. All of them are saying in reply: "Yes, your affirmation would be appreciated. Please don't take me for granted."

There is another reason people do not want to give praise and it has to do with competition. Competition prods us to push ahead and stay ahead as #1. In the process of pushing and staying ahead, we may not be inclined to recognize someone else's achievements because they threaten our own. After all, if we praise another's talents, we may call the attention of others to them and in the process, we may call it away from ourselves.

How many times have we been in the presence of someone who refused to join in with a chorus of praise because of a gnawing sense of superiority that he or she would like to maintain? It's a sad spectacle.

Last, there is jealousy. Jealousy guards praise greedily and doles it out sparingly—or not at all.

This may be the most common stumbling block to praise. To be in the presence of someone whose gifts so outshine our own frequently leaves us deflated, depressed, and unable to praise. How can we praise when we feel so inadequate, resentful, and jealous?

It's not easy.

How can we praise someone else's achievements and victories when we don't see anything in our lives worthy of praise?

It's not easy.

How can we praise when someone else's gifts are exactly the gifts we wish we had—intelligence, poise, wit, wisdom, or whatever?

It's not easy.

And saddest of all, how can we praise God—*ever*—since God is responsible for having made us as we are, minus those gifts we think we need?

It may not be easy, but the alternative isn't easy, either. To live stingily and to begrudge praise is the way of misers and not of brothers and sisters who know what it means to be lavishly and unconditionally loved by the same Creator.

Third, we do not praise when we are concerned that praise induces pride.

The ancient Greeks singled out hubris, an inflated sense of self-worth and a false sense of invulnerability, as the most feared and despicable character flaw. More than that, hubris was an unforgivable sin, and whenever we come across it in Greek tragedy, we can rest assured that the hero who possesses it is doomed.

The purpose of identifying the sin of hubris was to serve justice— to affirm that the identity of those who thought they were mighty was with common people. Some of that same fear is ours today. There is a fear among us that pride causes us to lose our grip on reality and helps us to think we are someone we are not. In fact, one of the definitions of pride is "thinking too highly" of oneself. Usually, the fantasy of the proud person is that he or she is more talented or smarter than is actually so. Pride also often masks self-doubt and insecurity about one's true worth.

It could be that the fear of unreasonable and haughty pride is why Christianity, from the time of John Cassian and St. Gregory the Great, placed pride at the top of the list of the deadliest sins. Let there be no mistake about it: even among Christians, pride was to be avoided at all costs. We even popularized an axiom, "Pride goes before a fall."

The kind of pride that made someone feel superior and even equal to God was closely (and incorrectly) connected with praise. So, together with pride, praise became something to be avoided because it appeared to be the cause and the root of pride.

It seemed that the person who did not praise was doing a service for humanity!

The truth is that while there *is* a kind of pride that is a vice, there is also a kind of pride that is a virtue.

Pride of the second variety is the emotion captured in the British film *Chariots of Fire,* when two runners in the 1924 Berlin Olympics, Eric Liddell and Harold Abrahams, exceeded their own expectations. In their triumph, we saw pride in the faces of those who watched. We saw it in the shake of the fist and the toss of the head as a runner crossed the finish line. We felt exhilarated that these men were able to do what they did.

Yet even Eric Liddell's sister, Jennie, had her moment of doubt about what the achievement and adulation would do to her brother. Unlike his sister, Liddell understood his accomplishments at the Olympics as connected with his mission and faith in life. "I believe God made me for a purpose, for China, but He also made me fast. And when I run, I feel His pleasure. To give it up would be to hold Him in contempt. . . . To win is to honor Him." The pride Liddell felt as "gift" was appreciated in the context of the Giver of the gift. When praise is involved with pride that elevates the spirit and acknowledges the Giver, it is a very fitting response.

There is also the pride that we witness when a young father and mother behold their baby's first efforts at smiling or walking or talking. The pride is out of proportion to the ordinariness of the event, but the occasion is one of bliss for the parents.

These situations of verbal and non-verbal pride call for praise. We want to praise the athletes for their achievements and mastery, and we expect the parents to praise their toddler's wobbly steps.

The fear that praise will lead to the vice of pride is severely exaggerated; it is most likely unjustified. It seems far better to live in fear of not praising enough and of not sharing accomplishments and joys and milestones with our loved ones than to worry about inflating someone's ego with too much praise.

Other difficulties arise when we speak of praising God. C. S. Lewis acknowledged that praising God was a stumbling block for him after his conversion to Christianity. Either God is self-sufficient and not in need of praise—especially from creatures—or God suffers from an inadequacy that corresponds to the deficiency of rock stars and body builders who need to be told, over and over again, how great they are.

Lewis resolved his dilemma by recognizing that "when we do not praise God, the loss is ours, not God's, for we deny ourselves as regards the supremely Valuable, what we delight to do, what indeed we can't help doing, about everything else we value." The point is that we all lose when we do not praise. We all win when we do.

Fourth, we do not praise the giver when we feel the gift was due us. This obstacle to praise was made very real to me several summers ago when two retired couples from our neighborhood visited their children for family reunions commemorating 50th wedding anniversaries. By Labor Day, I had caught up with each couple and heard about the celebrations.

One couple came back from Texas with a new car from their children and grandchildren. The wife said: "It's about time they did something for us! After all these years, it's the least they could do." The husband felt much the same way. "They gave us a stripped-down model: no air conditioning and no stereo," he said. The second couple spoke in awe of each of their children's and grandchildren's achievements and showed me the prize souvenir of the trip: a collage of photographs they had framed to remember a milestone event in their family's history.

One couple could not bring themselves to praise because they felt they deserved everything they received. In their words, "It was about time." They had so calculated the return on their investment that they knew they deserved more (at least power windows). By contrast, the other couple counted on nothing except the company of loved ones at their anniversary, and that presence was gratefully and graciously received.

The first couple was self-centered, not other-centered. And self-centeredness is a major impediment to praise. A stance so emphatically turned in on the self blocks the ability to notice others and to behold what others are doing. It is precisely in the beholding that praise becomes possible; without beholding, praise never gets off the ground.

Praise happens when we step out of the way and attend to the detail of another. If the ego is not pushed aside, if we are convinced that we deserve what we are given—or worse, that we deserve *more* than we are given—then we cannot experience that which begs to be seen, heard, touched, noticed, and honored.

The first couple thought only of themselves, and what they lost was far more than power windows.

A fifth reason we are not effective praisers is that we are suspicious of emotions. A long tradition encourages us to separate emotions from reason and then to favor reason. Restraint emerges as a virtue, and love and overflow—those constants of praise—are devalued.

The emotions connected with praise have also been used, abused, and overused to flatter people and to manipulate them, thus making us wary of praise, which too often seems insincere. Take a look at the sports pages to track the emotional frenzy of fans when a championship is within grasp. But fans are fickle. Their cheers evaporate when the winning streak ends. And those who watch from the sidelines learn indelible lessons about the mercurial temperaments of some praisers.

Advertising, with its relentless anthems in praise of "the sturdiest aluminum foil," "the chunkiest candy bar," and "the most flavorful dog food," all too readily conditions us into thinking that all praise is false or is at least overblown. Many potential praisers refrain from praise because of the difficulty of making praise sound genuine and different from the praise given to refrigerators, deodorants, and yogurt.

When praise is heaped in trivial ways, it loses all power when an appropriate subject for adoration comes into view. Thomas Merton's judgment seems right on target:

> Praise is cheap today. Everything is praised. Soap, beer, toothpaste, clothing, mouthwash, movie stars, all the latest gadgets which are supposed to make life more comfortable—everything is constantly being "praised." Praise is now so overdone that everybody is sick of it, and since everything is praised with the official hollow enthusiasm of the radio announcer, it turns out in the end that *nothing* is praised.

The fear of the hollowness identified by Merton prompts us, when we are on the receiving end of praise, to weigh it for authenticity, flattery, and connivance. Even sound and healthy people look for hidden agendas when they are affirmed. Praise from men is often suspect by women who have trusted compliments in the past only to be deceived. Praise from women is often suspect by men who wonder whether some calculating female is baiting a trap. In these situations, praise cannot be offered without misgivings, nor can it be accepted with honor.

When the theologian John Shea probes the place in us from which we might prefer to praise, one discovery he makes is alarming. The sad truth, according to Shea, is that many of us feel more comfortable with emotions that flow from self-abnegation and self-criticism and less comfortable with those that emerge from our own sense of honor, trust, self-worth, integrity, and magnanimity of spirit. What makes this observation particularly troubling is that the preference is not occasional but habitual. Shea writes that many "people fear soaring. They can never get into Francis of Assisi's canticle to the sun. Most people can deal with prayer out of experiences of diminishment, but not out of experiences of power." An attitude that allows us to pull out all the stops—to soar, to surrender, and to celebrate—remains unknown to potential praisers who keep the brakes on their emotional lives and never praise, or live, at full throttle.

And finally, sometimes we don't praise because we don't see anything to praise. This could be the saddest of all reasons for not praising. It has to do with a blindness that keeps us from seeing both the gift and the giver.

Not to praise someone or something worthy of praise doesn't lessen the subject. An excellent ballet still remains an excellent ballet; a stunning contralto remains stunning, even if she doesn't stun us. *Not praising lessens us.* The pitiful loss is always ours because our obstinate actions shrink our vision of the universe.

When all is said and done, opportunities to praise are graces to us. Our responses to these privileged moments elevate and expand us. C. S. Lewis once observed: "Except where intolerable adverse circumstances interfere, praise almost always seems to be inner health made audible." He may never have written a truer word.

BENEFITS OF PRAISE

The profile of the praiser is so attractive and healthy that it stands in sharp contrast to the closed and conflictive person who does little or no praising. To praise brings a number of benefits.

Praisers are receptive, not closed, people. Their outlook is broadened, they take more in, their senses become more attuned to the unique, the beautiful, the honest, the praiseworthy. So much of the world, and the God who created it, becomes the occasion for genuine enjoyment, astonishment, and praise. People who praise are interesting; those who do not are boring.

People who praise cultivate healthy and mutually helpful relationships. Because they are unthreatened by other people, praisers have an extended capacity to receive persons and events at the same time that they invite those others to be themselves. People who do not praise cannot reach out to others but prefer instead to talk about themselves, their accomplishments, their interests, their worth, their dreams, their everything.

This is also boring. *Very boring.*

People like to be near people who praise. (Scripture tells us that God likes to be near them, too.) Honest praisers are supportive and generous and appreciate both who people are and what people do. Praisers are sensitive, alert, and ready to find something positive to praise. Praisers uplift people's spirits because it becomes evident that the praise bestowed comes from truth. Critical people are crabby and oppressive. Praisers are joyful and alive.

Not only do people like to be near praisers, but people near praisers also tend to produce more and become more effective, according to the authors of *The One-Minute Manager.* They live up to their potential; they live out the truth of our claims for them. Parents who praise their children (as well as employers who praise co-workers, and so on) know how very true this advice is.

Our prayer life is invigorated by praise because we let our spirits soar. This is not a small benefit. Praise allows us to pull out all the stops, to celebrate, and not to fear joy.

Praisers learn that Jesus praised and gave glory to God because of the Spirit in his life. The Spirit in our own lives will allow us to do the same. To praise is to honor the presence of the Spirit of God within us and within the one being praised.

Praising exercises our eyes. What we see dimly and through a glass darkly comes alive through praise. We see with new appreciation. We see in Technicolor. We learn not only that God is everywhere but also how to uncover God's handiwork. Annie Dillard, the Pulitzer Prize–winning author, did this at Tinker Creek. There she found in "the coot's feet, the mantis' face, a banana, the human ear" evidence that "not only did the creator create everything, but that he is apt to create *anything.*"

Here are some suggestions for overcoming obstacles that often stand in the way of praise. They are not hard-and-fast rules, so treat them lightly and with no sense of obligation.

TO EXERCISE PRAISE

---

1. *Remember that Jesus praised.* So did John the Baptist (see Luke 3:16), Mary, Paul (see Phil. 4:8), Elizabeth (see Luke 1:42), and innumerable other people in the Bible. Their example tells us that true praise isn't improper, or prideful, or un-Christian. These major role models in the Scriptures praised and inspire us to follow their example.

2. *When a reason to praise comes into view, we need to seize the moment.* Waiting until the next performance evaluation or class reunion, or until we write our Christmas cards or the event is repeated, lets the present and proper moment slip through our fingers.

3. *Keep a diary or a journal of persons and/or things you wished you had praised during the course of the day.* Take time to remember those persons and things at the end of the day . . . give thanks and praise . . . and take the appropriate step to let them know about it. Make a telephone call or drop someone a note to tell someone that he or she did a fine job. Be specific about what you are praising. And be accurate.

4. *Avoid the trap of offering phony praise.* Phony praise always sounds like phony praise. "Praise singing is like love," Simonides says in Mary Renault's novel *The Praise Singer.* "You do it from the heart, or you're a whore."

5. *Praise children.* Grandchildren, great-grandchildren, students, friends' children, and neighbors' children blossom when they are affirmed. Don't miss this opportunity to be part of their lives. It is also true that when we affirm children, they learn the *importance* of praising and may become better praisers themselves.

6. *Make a list of those persons you live with or near for whom you can find nothing to praise. With the help of others, try to learn things about them worthy of admiration.* Collect data until you make it your own: be sure not to praise unless it is sincere.

7. *Get in the habit of praising God regularly simply for who God is as well as for what God has done in your life.* Take time to notice the activity of God in the world today. Notice and wonder—and allow yourself to be amazed.

8. *Make a conscious point to begin prayer by praising God.* "It is good to give thanks to the Lord" (Ps. 92:1); "Let everything that breathes praise the Lord" (Ps. 150:6). Too often, our prayers begin by asking for favors.

9. *When praising others is particularly difficult, remember that you are accepted by God not by virtue of being #1, but because you are a daughter or son of God.* Take time and let God accept and affirm you so that you will lessen your need to be #1.

10. *Don't save praise for special occasions.* Praise for large and small gifts, big and little surprises. It's a great way to cultivate the habit of praise.

11. *Enjoy the company of people who affirm you.* We all need praise and we owe it to ourselves to live in supportive climates. It is hard to imagine that one who is not praised can extend it to others.

12. *Develop your own style of praise.* Observe how different people praise, and experiment with styles until you find one that you like. Praise that is direct is usually communicated more effectively than praise that is circuitous. "That was a wonderful solo" is better than "All of the soloists in the series were good, and so were you, of course." Be sensitive to timing. There are moments that are opportune for praise, but there are other moments that are too rushed and frazzled for praise to be welcomed, absorbed, or even heard.

The most important thing is to get into the habit of praise. Style can be perfected and timing can almost always be improved. An awkward attempt is better than no attempt at all. Take one step at a time and make it a personal goal to be a praiser in the footsteps of the One who showed us that praise is all about being fully alive.

NOTES

The epigraph comes from Alice Walker, *The Color Purple* (New York: Harcourt Brace Jovanovich, 1982), 167.

Information from Ken Blanchard and Spencer Johnson is found in their book *The One-Minute Manager* (New York: Berkley Books, 1982).

Claus Westermann's observation about life and praise is found in *Praise and Lament in the Psalms,* translated by Keith R. Crim and Richard N. Soulen (Atlanta: John Knox Press, 1981), 159.

For the Augustine quotation, see St. Augustine, *The Confessions,* Book I, Chapter 1 (New York: Penguin Books, 1966), 21.

The quote from Samuel Johnson and several other observations on praise were provided to me by Robert Langworthy.

C. S. Lewis is cited several times in this chapter. In all cases, the source is his *Reflection on the Psalms* (New York: Harcourt Brace Jovanovich, 1958), 90–98.

The original source for Karl Barth's quote regarding praise as an endangered undertaking is his *Credo,* translated by J. Strathearn McNab (London: Hodder & Stoughton, Ltd., 1968), 14. I found Barth's remark cited in Westermann's book *Praise and Lament in the Psalms,* cited above, 5.

The encounter between Celie and Shug is found in Alice Walker's novel *The Color Purple,* cited earlier, 167–168.

For the ideas on the distinctions between thanking and praising, see Claus Westermann, cited earlier, 27–30.

The statistics on 60 days of nagging for each school year come from an article in *Educator's Newsletter* cited in the *New York Times* (National Edition), August 23, 1988, 22.

The legendary coach Vince Lombardi believed in maintaining and enforcing discipline in a perfect manner. A player reported of him that "in the first week of practice Lombardi yelled so long and so loud he lost his voice." On Lombardi, see articles in the *New Yorker,* December 8, 1962, 213–230; *Time,* December 19, 1960, 43; and *Newsweek,* January 29, 1968, 75. From the *Newsweek* article: "Thus team members show up for meetings ten minutes early, hesitate to take a sip of water during practice in case it should be interpreted by 'Coach' as a sign of weakness and often play with the kind of injuries that send other pros to the hospital."

For a helpful discussion of jealousy and pride, see Willard Gaylin, M.D., *Feelings* (New York: Harper & Row, 1979), 77–88.

Chariots of Fire, a Warner Brothers and Ladd Co. film release, 1981, is the source of the quotes about and by Eric Liddell.

Thomas Merton's humorous remarks concerning praise come from his book *Praying the Psalms* (Collegeville, MN: The Liturgical Press, 1956), 10.

John Shea's comments concerning experiences of diminishment and experiences of power can be found in "A Storyteller's Story of Prayer," in Betty and Art Winter's *Stories of Prayer* (New York: Sheed & Ward, 1985), 42.

Annie Dillard, *Pilgrim at Tinker Creek* (New York: Bantam Books, 1975), 138, is the source of the quote about God creating anything.

Mary Renault, *The Praise Singer* (New York: Pantheon Books, 1978), 95, is the source of Simonides' quotation.

Chapter 3

EATING

So, whether you eat or drink, or whatever you do,
do everything for the glory of God.
1 CORINTHIANS 10:31

For as long as I can remember, once my children were old enough to understand, the holiday season officially began with a reading of Truman Capote's "A Christmas Memory." Each November, we listened as the pre-adolescent narrator Buddy and his sixty-something woman friend scrounged for nickels and dimes to buy ingredients for the fruitcake they would make for their favorite people, including the president of the United States, Franklin Delano Roosevelt, and his wife, Eleanor.

No one in our family liked or ever made fruitcake, but the enthusiasm of the pair marked for us the beginning of a favorite series of preparations for Christmas, those having to do with food and eating. Nose-tingling odors saturated our kitchen as canisters of homemade rum pudding cooled on the countertops. Hot mulled apple cider was always just an elbow away, and the aroma of the cinnamon, orange peel, and cloves with which we laced it suffused the house, drifting out to the world whenever we opened a door.

Once in a while a relative clucked sympathetically at the fuss involved in getting set for the big feast that gathered the family at our house. But for us it was no trouble at all.

We knew instinctively that there is power in the symbol of food: food prepared, food shared, food as a source of strength and warmth, food as a measure of hospitality and generosity, food as opportunity for healing, food that bonds families and invites strangers to friendship; eating as an occasion to socialize, as a place of gratitude for God's bounty, and as defining ("we are what we eat") our very selves. To live without food is not only to deprive the body of essential nourishment and proper pleasure—it is also to deprive the spirit of its need for relationship. To live without food is to die twice.

The correlation between body and spirit may be most apparent in this exercise. The healing and strengthening of both happens best at meals prepared with care.

WE ARE WHAT WE EAT

It is no wonder that the major religions of the world all grant special significance to food and eating. Muslims fast at Ramadan, Jews gather for the Seder, Christians celebrate the Eucharist, and Hindus offer food for the gods. While dietary regulations sometimes can become idolatrous, religion tells us that our spiritual constitution is influenced by our physical well-being (or lack of it), and vice versa. Food is seen as the bridge that connects the material and spiritual worlds. The simple truth, as John Carmody has written from the Christian perspective, is that "through our bodies we are spirits-in-the-world, significantly shaped by what we eat."

The correlation between diet and disposition, nutrition and neuroses, and health and happiness has directed religious leaders to speak of food and eating with some frequency. John Wesley, the founder of Methodism, published a tract called *A Primitive Physic* on simple remedies to cure most diseases and offered the following advice:

Water is the wholesomest of all drinks.

Coffee and tea are extremely hurtful to people who have weak nerves.

At the other end of the spectrum, Gandhi wrote of fasting not merely as a regimen to foster health but also as a spiritual exercise of self-restraint and solidarity with the oppressed.

Cultures complement the wisdom of religious thought in valuing food for the health and well-being that it can bring. For centuries Japan emphasized vegetables and cereal grain as mainstays of its diet before it adopted a Western fondness for beef (and increased its mortality rate from heart diseases in the process). Traditional dietary customs reinforced preferences for foods that were nutritionally sound—for example, corn for the American Indian and rice for Asians. Those of us with parents, grandparents or great-grandparents from the "Old Country" know the careful preparations "from scratch" that went into meals filled with nutrients (and sometimes too many calories as well!). We tend to sacrifice that by eating prepackaged versions bolstered with artificial colors and tastes.

DIETARY ANARCHY

Over the years, the fundamental insight of religion and culture has faded. Although we in the modern West have extended our life spans by conquering infectious diseases through scientific discoveries like antibiotics, immunizations, and improved sanitation, we have not improved our diets. Eating disorders abound in our society. We are obsessed with food but are without a healthy relationship to it. Obesity is America's leading ailment and anorexia and bulimia are a growing problem for others who choose destructive means to achieve weight loss. Eating disorder clinics have sprung up at hospitals and on college campuses across America to help those who are out of control with food and drinking addictions.

The dietary anarchy that pervades our culture is associated with fatigue, mental depression, aches and pains, high and low blood pressure as well as other circulatory problems, cancer, stroke, diabetes, and degenerative diseases of the organs, to name only a few. And this is only the top layer of our worries.

According to nutritionist Jane Brody, more than 500 new food products, most nutritionally deprived, appear annually for consumers to purchase. It is difficult to discriminate the "jewels" from the "junk." Routine surveys show only a fraction of the population is able to describe a nutritionally balanced meal.

SOME EAT, SOME STARVE

On the other side of these fears lies a correlative tragedy. Rich Christians (and rich members of other religions, too) eat more than their fill while hunger and starvation ravage our world. The horror is unveiled with unrelenting regularity in one report after the next: some overeat while others starve.

Poverty in the developing nations as well as in significant pockets of the United States and other industrialized countries produces illiteracy, disease, and death. At least one billion people experience the anguish of poverty daily. Some are found in our own cities scavenging from dumpsters. Mothers beg to feed their children. And some children in the United States lucky enough to go to school do so without having eaten breakfast that morning or dinner the night before.

We need to return to the wisdom of Christianity as we unravel the interconnected crises facing us. Christianity has traditionally held keys to insight and guidance in the areas of food and eating. Redeeming humanity depends on exercising wiser options regarding the food we eat, its production and distribution, and its religious significance.

PARADISE LOST AND FOUND

In the beginning, food was intended as a healing, nourishing, and bonding agent. That bond was broken by the disobedience of Adam and Eve in Eden. Adam and Eve introduced us to the toxic capabilities of food. Not only were we condemned from that point on to work for our food by the sweat of our brows, but we also had to deal with violent weather and uncooperative soil in its production. Then

Jesus, the New Adam, gave us a new bond to God through food when he identified himself with bread at his farewell dinner. The paradise lost by Adam and Eve in an act of disobedience connected with food was restored by Jesus Christ in an act of obedience connected with food.

When Jesus assumed a fragile human body, he became as dependent on food as we. And he came from a tradition that valued food and family and saw them intrinsically connected.

About the food Jesus ate, we can make some relatively safe assumptions that his diet included fish, bread, lamb, olives, and cheese. One authority suggests that it was "probably low in fat, high in fish, grains and fiber." The gospel accounts record that Jesus was tired, frustrated, and weary, but there is no mention of him being in poor health. He appears to have been physically fit, with high levels of vitality characterizing his ministry.

The Jewish traditions of Passover and unleavened bread would have figured prominently in Jesus's meals. The remembrance of God's saving deeds became ritualized in these feasts where the act of eating lamb and unleavened bread in a family setting enabled the chosen people to feed on the memory of their deliverance from the hands of the pharaohs of Egypt. Likewise, the sojourn in the desert focused for the Israelites their dependency on Yahweh for food and water. Yahweh quenched thirst and provided daily bread (Exod. 16:13–36) in the form of manna, which "was like coriander seed, white, and the taste of it was like wafers made with honey" (v. 31).

THE WOLF AND THE LAMB FEED TOGETHER

The ritual remembrances of these miracles and the internalization of God's providential care as breadwinner encouraged the Hebrews to think of the Promised Land as a place overflowing with food. Isaiah wrote about it this way: "On this mountain the Lord of hosts will make for all peoples a feast of rich food, a feast of well-aged wines" (25:6). This feasting prefigured the banquet at the end of the world where the faithful would be welcome regardless of class or status and the hard-hearted would be sent away with empty stomachs (Isa. 65:13). In that new heaven and new earth, the sign of ultimate peace was expressed in terms of harmonious food arrangements even in the animal kingdom: "The wolf and the lamb shall feed together, the lion shall eat straw like the ox" (Isa. 65:25).

With such a conscious (and perhaps unconscious) appreciation of food and its symbolism in his background, it is no wonder that Jesus referred to food as often as he did and regarded it so frequently as the sign of presence and solidarity. The Last Supper was one in a long series of meals Jesus hosted or was present at as guest in the gospel accounts. But there were many in out-of-the-way places before that memorable meal. Even *after* the resurrection (John 21:9–14), Jesus hosts a meal, described in a recent book:

> It is lakeside, beautiful to picture. The sun is rising. The disciples have fished all night and they are tired and their stomachs are empty. When they come ashore, they see a charcoal fire, with fish on it, and some bread. There, wreathed in the smell of food cooking out-of-doors at dawn, stands the Crucified and Risen Christ, the person whom Saint John identified in his introduction as the Logos, the Word through whom all things were made. He says to them (and I believe he says to each of us at the beginning of every day):
>
> "Come and have breakfast."

COMMUNITY SAYS WE ARE NOT ALONE ANYMORE

Jesus understood how a meal functioned in human affairs—how it gathered together a community, how it reflected hospitality and how it invited disclosure. The meal became the metaphor that uncovered these themes of community, hospitality, and disclosure and placed them front and center in the Gospel of Jesus Christ.

Food nourishes our physical existence and sustains our spirits. Most people prefer not to eat alone; having to do so is frequently considered a privation, according to Jesuit theologian Thomas Clarke. "Even prisoners are permitted, with some risk to institutional order and security, to share meals, and it may be the most oppressive aspect of solitary confinement that one has no companion to break bread with." The social activist Dorothy Day linked human contact with the food served at Catholic Worker soup kitchens. "We know each other in the breaking of the bread, and we are not alone anymore. . . . Life is a banquet . . . even with a crust, where there is companionship," Day wrote.

Often a meal gathers people around a table. Jesus gathered around a table with the poor, those of dubious reputation, and the socially unacceptable, and then suggested that our preference ought to mirror his. It is amusing to note the admittedly dated advice of Emily Post in planning a dinner party. To guarantee a memorable evening with charming guests, Emily Post advised that "the hostess who gathers in all the oddly assorted frumps on the outskirts of society cannot expect to achieve a very distinguished result." Jesus saw other possibilities in the mix.

The status of the hosts or guests at meals mattered very little to Jesus. He ate with the well-connected and the unhinged yet indicated a preference for dining with those who most needed him.

The religious establishment, on the other hand, was frequently upset over Jesus's choice of table companions. Their common understanding of being invited into the intimacy of someone's "home" suggested that by accepting such an invitation one was approving or even participating in the reputation of the host. When that reputation was scurrilous, an innocent person like Jesus would be tainted by it.

Jesus, however, offered a different interpretation of his behavior. When he ate at the home of the tax collector Levi (Luke 5:29–32), he did not see his host influencing his moral vision as much as he saw himself influencing his host. In other words, Levi would not bring Jesus into complicity with evil; Jesus would bring Levi into complicity with good.

The message passed on to the disciples was simple. Like Jesus, they were not to fear contamination by sinners but rather were taught that the good news was powerful enough to transform sinners.

LAZARUS: ONE WHOM GOD HELPS

And when it came to the poor, there were to be places reserved especially for them. In fact, Jesus suggested that the rich who could invite us in return be received *after* the beggars, the crippled, the blind and the otherwise disabled (Luke 14:12–14) who would be less likely to return the favor. He told the story of the rich man Dives and the beggar Lazarus to reinforce this point (Luke 16:11–31). "Dressed in purple and fine linen," the rich man "feasted sumptuously every day" while Lazarus would have been happy "with what fell from the rich man's table." The rich man failed to see Lazarus's hunger, and that kind of sinful neglect disturbed the God of the poor.

Even if he did not deliberately refuse to give Lazarus the crumbs he sought, the rich man's callousness was intolerable. In this matter of sharing food and drink, God promised to balance the books at a final reckoning when the hunger of the poor man Lazarus (and all other poor men and women) would be eased by none other than God, while Dives (and all other selfish rich men and women) would suffer. The meaning of the name *Lazarus,* "one whom God helps," underlines God's protective stance vis-à-vis the poor.

SOUL FOOD

From a Christian point of view, every shared human meal is a partial realization of the ultimate communion to which all humans are called. For the gathering on earth to be transparent to the gathering at the messianic banquet, it must reflect a universality of participants, where a place is reserved for everyone, even those deemed unworthy in the eyes of some. We are on safe ground only if our call to the table reminds us of our responsibility to the hungry. The final judgment will hinge on how widely we extend the invitation, how faithfully we share our daily bread, how much we serve and *are* soul food.

The sadness the Apostle Paul records from Corinth (1 Cor. 11:27–34) was that when the community gathered to celebrate the meal of remembrance, the first arrivals did not wait for others, so some went hungry. The Corinthians were guilty of turning the Lord's Supper into their own supper and not discerning the body in their midst. This sort of divisiveness is not peculiar to the early Church. At least one contemporary theologian has written of the distortions and deformations that have occurred within eucharistic practice even now.

The provocative thesis of the Asian theologian Tissa Balasuriya is that when there are eucharistic services for blacks and whites separately, as happens in some provinces of South Africa, the fundamental unity that this meal proclaims is profoundly violated. He also notes that what is sometimes true of South Africa is also sometimes true of the rest of the world even though the situation in other settings "may not be so blatantly revolting." Father Balasuriya writes: "Such divisions and injustices are an obstacle to the truthfulness of the celebration of the Eucharist. . . . While everywhere in the world society is deeply divided, especially between the rich and the poor, the powerful and the weak, the exploiting and the exploited, the Eucharist as a sacrament of unity . . . is a remedy against selfishness."

The only dependable power for life lies beyond all human structures and relationships. The same can be said of table fellowship, of the meal.

If any human meal is a sign of the gathering of a reconciled humanity, the power of the symbol comes from a faith that confirms this. A faith that honors the truth that "because there is one bread, we who are many are one body," is faith indeed (1 Cor. 10:17). Amazing but true.

"THE GIFT WITHOUT THE GIVER IS BARE"

Hospitality begins with an invitation. A host offers to share his home, to welcome another, to extend "self." A good hostess provides shelter, food, and companionship and treats the guest as one worthy of attention and care. The host needs an attitude of poverty, according to pastoral theologian Henri Nouwen. When the host is filled with ideas, prejudices, and worries, there is no room for the guest to relax, unwind, and be herself. The good hostess is a person who is empty enough (thus "poor" enough) to receive a guest.

The place of the host or hostess and the role of hospitality is an essential one when it comes to meals. James Russell Lowell wrote that what counts is "not what we give but what we share/For the gift without the giver is bare." It is in the hospitality extended at meals, especially meals in one's home, that the gift and giver meet as one.

I experienced this in a touching way several years ago when I visited the housekeeper who helped care for my children when they were little. In the four years since I had seen her, Manna (a curious name in a chapter on food!) had returned to her home in Warsaw, Poland, where she was married with two beautiful children.

In spite of my hesitation, Manna and her husband insisted that I have dinner at their apartment. I was reluctant because of the severe food shortages in Poland, having witnessed the long lines outside food stores and the empty shelves inside. And I remembered the stories about scarcity that Manna had shared while she lived with us.

I accepted with misgivings, yet Manna prepared a feast: potato pancakes, roast pork, homemade noodles, sauerkraut, cake, coffee. When the supply of any item was small, every member of the family at the table took a tiny portion and ushered the serving platter into my hands so that I would have my fill. Their joy in providing for me and the lavishness of their hospitality was so sincere and gracious that the evening became one of those rare and truly unforgettable lifetime memories.

In the Rule of St. Benedict lies this nugget: "All guests who present themselves are to be welcomed as Christ . . . " (53:1). But far more impressive than the loftiness of that counsel is the item in Benedict's instruction for the porter: "As soon as anyone knocks, or a poor man calls out, he replies 'Thanks be to God' and then with all gentleness . . . provides a prompt answer with the warmth of love" (66:3–4). Manna and her family embodied both counsels, with special merit for the second, which is far more difficult than the first. For what the porter is asked to do is to welcome guests (even unexpected ones) by being fully present to them, welcoming them around the table. That kind of openness and hospitality is possible only when we are at ease with ourselves—"at home in our own house"—actually and metaphorically speaking. The gift of hospitality allows another to be completely himself or herself and starts with peace in the host's heart.

St. Benedict's rule tells us balance is the key. We are called to provide openness and warmth but not to smother our guest. Moderation is the clue. The story of Mary and Martha in the Scriptures (Luke 10:38–42) provides us with a vision of what it looks like when someone goes overboard extending herself and then regrets it—or at least grumbles about it. Hospitality that makes us feel awkward and uncomfortable is not true hospitality. Jesus refers to Mary's easy style in the episode as "the better part." Perhaps what was better about it was that she made Jesus feel welcome and comfortable, which is, after all is said and done, the core of hospitality.

Jesus as Host and as Food

Jesus was, apparently, a superb host as well as a coveted guest at meal gatherings. On the road to Emmaus, he was both: initially he accepted an invitation to dine with two travelers going up to Jerusalem, but he apparently took over the host's role by breaking bread and sharing it.

It was at the Last Supper that Jesus was host *in excelsis*. The framework of this dinner was the Jewish Passover, but it also had distinctive accents. The ritual began in John's Gospel when Jesus washed the feet of the disciples—a humble gesture that exceeded the responsibility of the host, who could have provided merely the basin and towels for the guests to take care of themselves. For the meal itself, the host provided simple fare: the fruits of the earth and the work of human hands, bread and wine. Then something special happened. Jesus identified with the elements so that he not only provided food for his guests but became their food as well.

In other words, the guests at the Last Supper feasted on God. The God of the covenant became food and drink, flesh, bone, and blood to feed his guests and us. C. S. Lewis offers a down-to-earth explanation:

> God made us: invented us as a man invents an engine. A car is made to run on gasoline, and it would not run properly on anything else. Now God designed the human machine to run on Himself. He Himself is the fuel our spirits were designed to burn, or the food our spirits were designed to feed on. There is no other.

No other indeed. All other hungers and thirsts can be satisfied in human ways, but the deepest hungers of the human heart and soul are satisfied by the bread of life, by God.

As a woman who shares with other women (in countless cultures across the centuries) the responsibility for food and meal preparation, I find the activity of Jesus at the Last Supper particularly pregnant with meaning. For it is women who experience being food for others. The unborn in the womb and the infant at the breast are fed not only *by* the mother; the nourishment provided *is* the mother.

So women who have prepared food, set tables for meals, provided hospitality for families and friends, and who have actually been food for others are in a privileged position to relate to the experience of Jesus at the Last Supper and in the Eucharist. This is not to deny that men can do this vicariously, of course, but it is an experience far less direct than the woman's. Men can provide bread for the table, they can earn "bread," and certainly by virtue of Holy Orders (in some traditions exclusively) they can consecrate bread, but they do not experience the parallel correspondence between the gift of Jesus in the Eucharist as physical and spiritual nourishment and the experience of women as food for others.

In a related vein, historian Caroline Walker Bynum writes that there is clear evidence that food as a symbol was more important to women than to men in medieval times. Yet Ms. Bynum also notes how both male and female writers of the medieval period imaged Christ as a mother "nursing" her Church, thus claiming for Jesus a maternal disposition and reinforcing the insight that for Jesus to feed us we would have to borrow imagery with which we are most familiar. And that imagery is feminine.

THE MEAL AS PLACE OF DISCLOSURE

It is a combination of the meal itself, the home setting, the pleasure of receiving guests, and the close physical contact the meal provides that invites openness and disclosure. For host and guest alike, the possibility and even desirability of an exchange of some depth (sometimes inadequately referred to as "good conversation") is often unexpressed but always hoped for. It is the privilege of the one preparing the meal and presiding at the meal to create a primary ritual that enables many patterns of relationship (person to person, person to food, person to earth as source of food, person to absent guests without food) to exist. And it is a vital and creative act of the hostess to bring people together so that connections are made at levels of significance.

The table itself helps to gather people who may initially be strangers into contact with each other, a few feet apart, where gestures, facial expressions, and whispers can be seen and heard. A "family" forms around the table. The revitalization of body takes place through nutrients; the revitalization of spirit, through this community.

This is community, of course, in a very provisional sense. It is not the community labored at through commitment, struggle, and pain. Nor is it a community of permanence. But the meal, whether special or ordinary, has the symbolic ritual power to engage different persons in a dialogue where humanness is the common currency. This happens only when a human being feels safely surrounded by love, and the potential for that "surrounding" is powerfully present at meals.

The opposite also is true. To collect people around a table and to hurry through a meal is to miss the opportunity for conversation and disclosure. To leave the pot on the stove so that each family member can ladle out a separate portion, or to consume TV dinners where the television and not another human being "interacts" with the one who is eating, are further examples of dysfunctional mealtimes. So is the popular "power breakfast" (or lunch or dinner), which respects persons as deal makers and kingpins, not as brothers and sisters, or the popular "three martini lunch," which drowns any depth of disclosure (and there may indeed be some of that) in the haze of alcohol.

As a keen observer of our nation's mores, Charles Dickens wrote this about American mealtimes after a visit to the United States: "There is no conversation, no laughter, no cheerfulness, no sociality, except in spitting; and that is done in silent fellowship round the stove, when the meal is over. Everyone sits down dull and languid, swallows the fare . . . and having bolted his food in a gloomy silence bolts himself, in the same state." A contemporary update on this state of affairs is provided by theologian Nathan Mitchell, who writes that one of the "doubtful legacies of the 1980s is widespread acceptance of an aggressive in-your-face rudness as the appropriate stance for all social interactions including those of the table."

The responsibility of the good host or hostess is to ensure that this does not happen. The host does not want the food, or the tableware, or the table setting to dominate attention. Nor does the attentive hostess want to gather such a homogeneous collection of people that there is only room for narcissistic self-interest. And neither host nor hostess wants to deal with a strong, ego-driven guest who monopolizes conversation.

But it is not all the host's responsibility; for the making of even this temporary community around the meal table is dependent on each of those present respecting the other. Some claim "chemistry" as the necessary ingredient, and by that they mean the electricity and energy sparked by circumstances and people. But chemistry plays a very small part. Rather, it is the willingness, even when the chemistry collides, to befriend, gently, every person present, to move our egos out of the way, to learn something about ourselves, our limits, and our need for others. All of these things take practice. Some of these things may be painful. All of these things are a way of saying that we need to be empty before we can be fed either friendship or food.

Like the rest of us, Jesus used food and drink, and especially meal-time, to reveal himself and to allow others to do the same. He used a chance meeting at a well to engage a Samaritan woman in conversation about thirst and water and to claim his identity as "living water" that quenches thirst forever (John 4). The Last Supper provided the opportunity to manifest himself as "the bread of life" and to uncover the positive value of the material world by honoring (and identifying with) bread and wine. And at the home of two sisters during the preparation for a meal, he helped one of the women to her new self-understanding as disciple (Luke 10).

Sometimes, multiple manifestations happened. For example, at mealtime in the home of Simon the Pharisee (Luke 7), all of the main characters were revealed at the end of the story in surprising ways. We learned, for example, that the perfect host Simon was not so perfect after all, either as host or as judge of character. Clearly, Simon had failed to offer the basic amenities—water for his feet, an embrace of welcome—to Jesus, his guest. The woman who is introduced as a sinner is disclosed as a penitent loved and forgiven with prodigal graciousness. And Jesus, thought not to be too savvy in judging the wheat from the chaff by allowing the sinner to minister to him, is disclosed as a prophet who reads hearts and indicts hypocrites. "All in all," theologian Edmond Barbotin notes in his commentary on this passage, "there is a full reversal in the whole situation, for none of the main characters leaves the table with the same moral identity that had earlier been ascribed to them at the beginning." The meal has served once again to reveal people to each other in unexpected ways.

BABETTE'S FEAST AND OURS

"Babette's Feast," Isak Dinesen's simple short story, also tells of the power of the meal to gather, to reconcile, and to disclose people to each other.

The French Revolution and the deaths of her husband and only son force Babette to flee Paris and to earn her keep by cooking for two single sisters, Martine and Philippa, in the bleak landscape of Berlevaag in Norway. Since the death of their father, the dean of the Lutheran congregation there, the sisters have held together the poor and austere group he left behind.

Their decision to honor the dean's 100th anniversary coincides with news that Babette has won the Parisian lottery. Reluctantly they agree to Babette's request that she prepare and pay for the dinner herself, but frightened by the extravagance of the celebration, Martine and Philippa discreetly urge the flock to remain stoic and unmoved, no matter what is placed before them at the table.

The people invited to the dinner are a sorry lot. The spiritual temperature of the congregation since the death of the dean has deteriorated from ordinary gloom to calculated bitterness and cynicism. "Like a toothache," two old women nag each other for past transgressions; another older gentleman refuses to forgive a grievance committed against him, but instead lets it stick in his heart "like a deep-seated, festering splinter."

Before these people, a feast worthy of royalty is set. No one in the congregation is aware of Babette's full identity. Not merely a cook, Babette was the celebrated chef at the Café Anglais in Paris. The congregation also never imagines that the feast cost Babette all of her lottery prize.

A last-minute guest, General Lorens Loewenhielm, is added to the table. A former suitor of Martine's, the general has returned to this small town to visit an aged aunt. Bedecked with military honors and ribbons, he also intends to assure himself that his departure from Berlevaag thirty years before was indeed the wiser choice.

The guests are tentative at first. Suspicious of the bounty laid before them, they hold on to grudges that distance them from each other, and they remain faithful to their vow not to notice the food and drink. Gradually, however, they are reconstituted by the feast in body as well as soul. "Their hearts like their numb fingers thawed," Dinesen writes.

Though usually in Berlevaag people do not speak much while they are eating, this evening "tongues were loosened." The pettiness and obstinacy that characterized the guests moments before have vanished. Instead, they speak of this little community's willingness to share each other's burdens and of the miracle many Christmases ago when the fjord froze so the dean could travel to the village on the other side.

Instead of growing heavier because of the meal, they instead grow "lighter in weight and lighter of heart" the more they eat and drink. When they finish the meal and return to their homes, men and women make peace with each other and play in the snow like little children.

Unlike the other guests, General Loewenhielm recognizes the genius behind the feast. He also recognizes in this meal a metaphor for grace. Dizzy with this feast of the senses and the spirit, the general finds the sublime in this remote Norwegian hamlet and can claim through the feast and grace the same truth: anything is possible. Grace abounds. It is not limited by human imagination, to be found only where we want it or expect it. It is, on the other hand, infinite. It is even disclosed where our mistaken choices have led us. God, after all, gives second chances, often by gifting us again with what we once rejected.

The simple story tells of the power of the meal in everyday human life. Isak Dinesen includes this short story in a collection called *Anecdotes of Destiny.* And so it is. As "the greatest culinary genius of the age," who knew how to turn a dinner into a love affair where the body and spirit are united, Babette's destiny was to prepare the setting for new life and new relationships.

Is it too farfetched to imagine that you and I share a similar destiny?

BENEFITS OF THE EXERCISE OF EATING

The correlation between body and spirit may be most apparent with regard to eating. Not only is the body dependent on food for survival (one rather important benefit!), but also the spirit depends on the gathering of family and friends around the table at mealtime, or else it, too, shrivels and dies.

When eating is understood as a spiritual exercise, benefits are to be found everywhere. At the top of the list, the most obvious are these:

Eating—or more precisely, eating well, is an agent of reconciliation. The primary reconciliation needs to happen with our bodies, especially when our bodies have been abused or neglected through poor nutrition. Even without acute signs of neglect, however, the exercise of taking care of our bodies restores a sense of value to that part of our beings that has not often been treated kindly and with respect.

Healings of all kinds are available to us. First, there is the healing directly linked to nutrients in food. Calcium, zinc, iron, fiber, beta-carotene, and hosts of vitamins have the capacity to affect our bodies-minds-spirits when absorbed as part of a sane diet. The setting of the meal itself does the same as we are nourished by food prepared and served in the company of other people. Plutarch once said: "We invite each other not to eat and drink, but to eat and drink together."

Our senses are heightened. A meal becomes a feast, as it was for Babette's guests, where everything shone and every sense—taste, smell, touch, hearing, and sight—was reinvigorated.

We gain awareness of the injustice that exists in the production, allocation, and consumption of food worldwide. This is where it all begins—with a growing consciousness of the power of food and how it is used to feed citizens of some countries and deprive the citizenry in other places.

To Exercise Eating

---

1. *Make conversation the centerpiece at the table.* Turn off the TV, the radio, and if necessary, the telephone. Put away the newspaper. Talk about how the day went, whom you saw, whom you wish had seen, what you read, what you did. Share a joke, an idea, a memory. Share something! And be sure to include everyone in the conversation.

2. *Gather people around a table.* The symbolism of the meal—disclosure, relaxation, hospitality, human contact, community—are more visible when a table is part of the picture.

3. *Think twice before bypassing breakfast.* Nutritionists still claim breakfast is the most important meal of the day and the one that can invigorate us for the hours that follow. Veteran teachers can tell when students have skipped breakfast, eaten poorly (cold pizza from the night before is a favorite), or gorged on donuts or other sweets so that they are hyped on a sugar high before 9:00 A.M. Some adults fare no better. *Think breakfast!*

4. *Invite someone from a nursing home, or someone living alone, or a student away from home to your house for a holiday meal or Sunday supper, or take them along on a family outing.*

5. *Volunteer in a soup kitchen or in a bread line to serve food.* The experience often opens people to discover the power of food when it reaches the hungry. "Sometime in your life," the Jesuit peace activist Daniel Berrigan hopes that "you might see one starved man [and] the look on his face when bread finally arrives. . . . For that look on his face . . . you might be willing to lose a lot, or suffer a lot—or die a little, even."

6. *Cook an international cuisine every once in a while.* Begin with those related to the ethnic roots of your own family and then branch out and include others in your repertoire.

Jeff Smith, TV's "Frugal Gourmet," comments on how fortunate we are that the "melting pot" never succeeded in blending the many traditions that came to America's shores. As a result, many national dishes have been preserved. Try homemade lasagna, pierogi, couscous, scones, crème caramel, gefilte fish, tempura, moussaka, or wonton soup. Learn something of the history of the food and its people while you are at it.

7. *Prepare food alert to the sense of smell.* Savor the smell of freshly baked bread hot from the oven, or fried onions, or herbs accompanying a roast. Breathe deeply. Enjoy.

If you need prompting for this exercise, James Stevens authored a classic description of this experience when he wrote in *Paul Bunyan* of loggers who stayed in their bunks on Sunday morning until aromas

from the cookhouse overtook them and rendered them almost unconscious to the rest of reality:

> A logger who was shaving would take a deep breath
> of this incense, and the blood would trickle unnoticed
> from a slash in his cheek; another in his bunk, would
> let his pipe slip from his hand and enjoy ardent inhala-
> tions, blissfully unaware of his burning shirt.

Practice the effect of smell for yourself.

**8. *Eat a meal that represents the diet of someone living in poverty
as an act of solidarity.*** Have a party (in some circles, this is the chic
thing to do) and serve half your guests a menu from the Third World
and the other half a typical American dinner. When it's over, talk.

**9. *Prepare nutritious and eye-appealing foods for snacks and
break times at meetings.*** Whatever lip service we pay to good nutrition goes down the drain if we do not back it up with a good example.

**10. *Teach your children (or your children's children, or friends'
children) how to cook and how to bake.*** Be sure to include the boys as
well as the girls in this exercise. There is something magical to children about putting a lump of dough on a cookie sheet and minutes
later seeing the finished product emerge from the oven.

   If you cannot cook, ask a friend to teach you. Or enroll in a class
offered at the local YMCA, community center, or church.

11. Serve *food.* We have grown so accustomed to buffets, self-ser-
vice, and cafeteria-style settings for our meals that this exercise welcomes the opportunity to make real what the symbolism of a meal is
all about—giving of ourselves and inviting others to do the same. At
the Last Supper, Jesus not only prepared food, he also distributed it to
his guests. His example is the one we want to imitate.

   The Dalai Lama discovered as a young child his need to be connected with the Master of the Kitchen, who prepared his meals. The
young boy grew so fond of the kindly master that he desired a visual
connection with the one who brought his food, "even if it was only
the bottom of his robe visible through the doorway." Reflecting on
this childhood attachment, the adult Dalai Lama concluded that

perhaps "the act of bringing food is one of the basic roots of all relationships."

12. *Learn about nutrition.* Jane Brody, cited earlier, not only has written fine books, but she also writes a regular nutrition and health column for *The New York Times.* Your librarian can steer you to other good resources. Resist the advice of those who tell you that this field is too complicated to learn. You can handle it.

13. *Encourage your office, parish, civic group, or neighborhood community to consider a food pantry.* There are several ways to do this. One possibility is to offer food bought in bulk to needy families at discounted prices. Another way is to ask for donations of food from the sponsoring group to be distributed to elderly persons (and others) who would be unlikely and/or unable to visit the resource in person.

14. *Grow your own food.* Start small with two tomato plants or a few zucchini squash. Or find a small plot to share with like-minded neighbors and plant a victory garden, fostering creative contact with the earth.

15. *Pray before eating.* Pray real prayers that reflect gratitude, warmth, hospitality, and a genuine awareness of those who live without basic food needs.

Pray and live so that things may be different and that daily bread may be shared by all.

NOTES

Truman Capote's reminiscence "A Christmas Memory" can be found in *A Christmas Treasury,* edited by Jack Newcombe (New York: Viking Press, 1982), 36–46.

John Carmody's comment on "spirits-in-the-world" comes from *Holistic Spirituality* (Mahwah, NJ: Paulist Press, 1983), 65.

A helpful adaptation of John Wesley's tract *A Primitive Physic* appears in *Weavings* 2 (November–December 1987), 37–40. See also John Wesley, *The Works of John Wesley,* Vol. 14 (Grand Rapids, MI: Zondervan, 1972).

For Gandhi's thoughts on fasting, see Mohandas K. Gandhi, *Autobiography: The Story of My Experiments with Truth* (New York: Dover Publications, 1983), 295–297.

Michio Kushi, in "Food for Spiritual Development," a lecture delivered to a symposium of the World Parliament of Religions, provides the information about diets and our ancestors.

Jane Brody, *Jane Brody's Nutrition Book* (New York: Norton, 1981), 13 ff. Much of the information in this section of my text depends on the research of Ms. Brody.

On questions of hunger and politics see, for example, *Hunger 1992: Ideas That Work* (Washington, DC: Bread for the World Institute on Hunger and Development, 1992) for an excellent bibliography and staggering statistics. See also Ron Sider, *Rich Nations in an Age of Hunger: A Biblical Study* (New York: Paulist Press, 1977).

The observations about Jesus's diet were made by Frederick Aigner, "The Body of Christ and Our Bodies," in *Dialog: Journal of Theology* 27 (Summer 1988), 178–180.

Gregory Post and Charles Turner's book *The Feast* (San Francisco: HarperSanFrancisco, 1992) is the source of the meditation on John 21.

The comment on prisoners and meals appears in Thomas E. Clarke, S.J., "On the Need to Break Bread Together," in *Human Rights in the Americas: The Struggle for Consensus* (Washington, DC: Georgetown University Press, 1982), 215.

Dorothy Day's statement about knowing each other in the breaking of the bread is found in her autobiography, *The Long Loneliness* (New York: Harper & Row, 1981), 285.

For the Emily Post comment, see Emily Post, *Etiquette: The Blue Book of Social Usage,* new and enlarged edition (New York: Funk & Wagnalls, 1928), 255.

See Tissa Balasuriya, *The Eucharist and Human Liberation* (Maryknoll, NY: Orbis Books, 1979), 50–51.

Henri Nouwen writes about the host and hospitality in "The Poverty of a Host," 65–70, and "Hospitality," 1–28, in *Monastic Studies,* Vol. 10 (Pine City, NY: Mount Savior Monastery, 1974).

James Russell Lowell's poem "The Vision of Sir Launfal" is found in *The Poetical Works of James Russell Lowell* (Boston, MA: Houghton Mifflin, 1885), 111.

C. S. Lewis, in *Mere Christianity* (New York: Macmillan paperback edition, 1960), 39, is the source of the quotation about God as the fuel our spirits were meant to burn.

Caroline Walker Bynum's fascinating work *Holy Feast Holy Fast* (Berkeley, CA: University of California Press, 1987) is worth reading cover to cover. See especially Chapter 9, "Woman as Body and as Food," 260–276.

The insights concerning the table at meals come from Edmond Barbotin, *The Humanity of God,* translated by Matthew O'Connell (New York: Orbis Books, 1976).

The Charles Dickens quotation from his *American Notes* is found in M.F.K. Fisher, *Here Let Us Feast* (San Francisco, CA: North Point Press, 1986), 292.

Nathan Mitchell's comment can be found in "The Amen Corner," in *Worship* 66(4), July 1992, 357.

Barbotin on the dinner in the home of Simon the Pharisee is quoted from his book *The Humanity of God,* cited earlier, 282–283.

Isak Dinesen's short story "Babette's Feast" is found in *Babette's Feast and Other Anecdotes of Destiny* (New York: Vintage Books, 1988), 3–48.

Daniel Berrigan's comments can be found in his book *Love, Love, at the End* (New York: Macmillan, 1971), 114–115. I learned of this citation through Sharon Parks's article "The Meaning of Eating and the Home as Ritual Space," in *Sacred Dimensions of Women's Experience* (Wellesley, MA: Roundtable Press, 1988), 184–192.

Jeff Smith's comment about the failure of the "melting pot" to meld the cultures of our ancestors appears in his book *The Frugal Gourmet on Our Immigrant Ancestors* (New York: Morrow, 1990), 14–15.

M.F.K. Fisher (cited earlier) is the source of the James Stevens quote from *Paul Bunyan*. See Fisher, 266.

The information about the early life of the Dalai Lama comes from his book *Freedom in Exile: The Autobiography of the Dalai Lama* (New York: Harper Perennial, 1991), 19.

Chapter 4

WORKING

Most of us have jobs that are too
small for our spirit.
STUDS TERKEL, *WORKING*

Ben Cohen and Jerry Greenfield make ice cream for a living. But anyone who has stood in line at their store in Burlington, Vermont (as I have), for their August White Sale—when all "white" flavors like coconut, vanilla, White Russian, and white chocolate are discounted—knows this is no ordinary ice cream. Some customers claim they would walk ten miles for a sample of a flavor called chocolate chip cookie dough.

Ben and Jerry set even higher standards for their company than they do for their products. No one in management earns more than five times the salary of the lowest paid employee. And 1% of profit is given to a lobbying organization committed to redirecting part of the national defense budget to peace causes. Through Ben & Jerry's Foundation, 7.5 percent of pretax profits are donated to nonprofit organizations.

The Foodshare Commission of Hartford, Connecticut, one of the foundation's beneficiaries, uses Ben & Jerry's contribution for containers to carry surplus food from area restaurants, caterers, hotels, and cafeterias to emergency food sites. The Children's Defense Fund is on the receiving end of Ben & Jerry's largesse, prompting the 1992 slogan "Leave No Child Behind." Burch House in Littleton, New Hampshire, receives funds to provide safe shelter for people in emotional or psychological distress.

The social mission and consciousness raising are blended into the product. Proceeds from Rainforest Crunch ice cream are used to preserve the Amazonian rainforest by funding a nut-shellers' cooperative. The Passamaquoddy Indians harvest the berries used in Wild Maine Blueberry, and a New York bakery staffed by unemployed homeless people makes the brownies used in Chocolate Fudge Brownie ice cream. Ben and Jerry believe that opportunities like these can be found with little effort by other business people.

Ben & Jerry's operates on a two-part bottom line: "How much money is left over at the end of the year?" and "How have we improved life in the community?" But the fiscal bottom line hasn't suffered. Ben & Jerry's, which opened in 1979 in a converted gas station in Burlington, Vermont, grossed in excess of $97 million in 1991.

Most of us don't make ice cream for a living, but our living should, like Ben & Jerry's, involve a sense of mission and creativity. The exercises in this chapter will help lead us to work that gives meaning to our existence, open up channels for our creativity, and allow us to invest in activities that help humankind to a better world.

We spend a third of our lives working. If the work we do, the people we work with, the sense of mission we have, and the passion and attitudes we bring to and get from our work are large enough for our spirits, our physical and spiritual well-beings are enhanced. When our jobs crush the human spirit, or become an addiction, our bodies and souls suffer.

Ben & Jerry's Homemade, Inc., may seem out of synch with the experience of millions of people for whom work is drudging, stressful, or highly competitive. Ben & Jerry's testimony of work satisfaction contradicts what some of us think that the Bible says about work— that we are to earn our living in pain, not by having fun making ice cream.

Are the Scriptures responsible for this negative evaluation of work?

IS WORK A BLESSING OR A CURSE?

In one of the earliest biblical accounts, the author of Genesis 2:15 offers a positive understanding of work in the field. Adam is expected to "till it and keep it," but the expectation is not oppressive. Work, even in paradise, is part of human fulfillment.

God does not ask human beings to take over mindless labor, according to theologian Francis Fiorenza. Adam is not asked to work in the field solely to be at another's beck and call. Instead, Adam owns a field and is in charge. To be human and alive is to be in harmonious relation to the world and to be continuing God's creation.

A major shift occurs in the field of Adam's life as a result of sin. From then on, the positive and humanizing attitude toward work is overshadowed by hardship and difficulty. The sin of Adam causes tension. As a result of sin, humans must earn their bread by the sweat of their brows. God curses the ground and promises it will bring forth "thorns and thistles." From now on, God says, there will be obstacles to satisfaction, creativity, and joy in one's work.

Even so, work itself is not seen as punishment or a curse. Created by God, work remains good. What changes is our ability to see that work builds the kingdom and that we are co-creators with God. Many of the problems and struggles connected with work are still with us in our culture and time, even though the workplace and the worker are capable of redemption.

Work does not have to be a form of slavery. The key to redeeming work lies with the God who created us. The way back to pleasurable, satisfying work is to collaborate with that God.

DOES GOD WORK?

Genesis tell us how God works. The story of creation shows work on a cosmic scale: in one day "God created the great sea monsters and every living creature that moves of every kind . . . and every winged bird of every kind" (1:21). On another day, God decreed that "the earth bring forth living creatures of every kind: cattle and creeping things and wild animals of the earth" (1:24). The God in Genesis is energetic, inventive, and productive, according to Jesuit theologian John Haughey.

Yet for all its drama, this narrative of creation from the first chapter of Genesis seems to some people too antiseptic and detached. This account depicts a God who creates by decree: " 'Let there be light'; and there was light" (1:3). Let there be stars . . . Let there be earth. Majestically, and without emotion, the world is fashioned by a master architect.

The African-American writer James Weldon Johnson believes something is missing from this description. Johnson favors a more hands-on approach to the creation story. For him, God is neither aloof nor authoritarian. Rather, God is someone who works physically, is involved in what is created, and responds personally to what is made. This God throbs with excitement over what is birthing.

Johnson rewrites the Genesis story this way:

> *And God stepped out on space*
> *And he looked around and said:*
> *I'm lonely—*
> *I'll make me a world*
> *. . .*
> *Then God reached out and took the light in his hands,*
> *And God rolled the light around in his hands*
> *Until he made the sun;*
> *And he set that sun a-blazing in the heavens.*

So far so good. But God is still lonely, so the second layer of creation is added, the making of the human person.

> *Then God walked around*
> *And God looked around*
> *On all that he had made.*
> *He looked at his sun,*
> *And he looked at his moon,*

And he looked at his little stars;
He looked on his world
With all its living things,
And God said: I'm lonely still.
Then God sat down—
On the side of a hill where he could think;
By a deep, wide river he sat down,
With his head in his hands,
God thought and thought,
Till he thought: I'll make me a man!

But the crown of Creation, Adam, betrayed the Creator. The impact of that betrayal is twofold: we suffer in our relationship to God and we suffer in our relationship to work. It would take Jesus to restore the wholeness to work that God intended.

JESUS: WORK AS MISSION

In his first speaking role in the Scriptures, the young boy Jesus explains to his concerned parents that he was missing from them for some anxious time because he was about the Father's business (Luke 2:49). One way or another, he was involved in that "business" all of his life.

Jesus not only worked; he also was on a mission. The root of the word *mission* (*missio*) means being sent, and Jesus was sent by God to bridge humanity and divinity and restore the human race to its spiritual moorings. It was hard work, often exasperating, but work in which he was (and still is) passionately involved.

Jesus went about the work of salvation by reminding those who would listen that God was at work within them. He preached God's love and promise of everlasting life for those who threw in their lot with him. But this was not a job in the conventional sense. It lacked steady hours, a benefits package, and a salary, and Jesus was often exhausted after a full day, yet without a pillow and a bed to comfort him.

From the beginning, he evangelized with a group of raw recruits known as disciples. Their talents and effectiveness varied widely. Some were slow learners. A few expected preferential treatment in the next world. Many were afraid. One mutinied. Instead of decreasing Jesus's work load, the disciples sometimes increased it. The more perceptive among them caught onto Jesus's insight that partnership in the mission of God was directly related to believing in Jesus and in seeing Jesus himself as the work of God. To the extent that they trusted the One who sent them and invoked his spirit, they were able to minister. When their egos got in the way, the mission crumbled.

There were times when people outside the closely knit group of disciples collaborated with Jesus. The Samaritan woman at Jacob's well was one of them (John 4). This Jewish stranger confused her when he spoke of "living water" to quench her thirst forever (v. 10–14). But she caught on quickly and chose to be part of Jesus's mission. Her response was especially significant, given the fact she had been divorced five times and was currently living with a sixth "significant other" without benefit of matrimony. Yet she preached the good news of the reign of God and many came to believe because of her (v. 39).

Saul, the persecutor of Christians, was also initially outside the loop of Jesus's followers but came to labor on his behalf. Converted on the way to Damascus, Saul's name was changed to Paul. Because of him and a handful of others, the church would exist in the provinces of Galatia, Macedonia, Achaia, and Asia. Ironically, this tireless worker made clear in his letter to the Romans that salvation was based not on work—if one meant *only* the doing of good deeds—but on faith, which prompted the believer to serve the brothers and sisters met along the way.

Paul's insight would later polarize Protestants and Catholics during the time of the Reformation and beyond, one side arguing for "justification by faith" and the other for "justification by works." From Jesus's own lips the message was clear: "Not everyone who says to me, 'Lord, Lord,' will enter the kingdom of heaven, but only the one who does the will of my Father" (Matt. 7:21). The Letter of James drives the point home succinctly: "Faith by itself, if it has no works, is dead" (2:17).

Both faith and work are necessary in the life of the true believer. Work without faith is empty; faith without work, a sham.

WHAT COUNTS AS WORK?

If the Creator God works, and if Jesus carries on that work in his own ministry, the disciples of Jesus must contribute to a religious understanding of work. Three areas are in urgent need of attention:

- ✦ Our definition of work is impoverished. We need to redefine work as more than paid employment.

- ✦ We need to listen to E. F. Schumacher's advice and look not only at what the worker contributes to work but examine what work does to the worker.

- ✦ A religious perspective is also needed to identify injustices associated with work.

"Work is whatever we think work is," writes Miroslav Volf in his book *Work in the Spirit: Toward a Theology of Work*. When we enjoy our work, the line between work and play fades. Some people enjoy their paid employment so much they would work for free. For years, my mother has said this about the bookkeeping work she does. In her seventies, she still occasionally commutes by subway to 42nd Street in New York City as a paid worker. "But I'd do it if they didn't pay me a penny," she says.

Defining work also brings us face to face with gender issues. We live in a transitional period where conventional ways of defining work are no longer adequate as the sole frame of reference. Yet, new ways of talking about work have not yet fully taken hold.

For example, at a small dinner party recently, I asked two married friends, Ellie and Michael, when in their lives they worked the hardest.

Michael said he worked hardest when he started out in banking and was an apprentice to his father-in-law, the bank's president.

"Those were tough days," Michael explained. "I needed the affirmation of my father-in-law, but the personal relationship complicated my performance at work. It was very awkward."

After barely a five-second pause, Michael offered another story. "Actually, the work I remember most was the five-year period we spent in Sydney, Australia. The work was hard but very rewarding. The friendships Ellie and I made through that assignment are still among our closest."

He quickly related another story. And then another. The stories were interesting and went on for an hour or more.

Finally, Ellie spoke. She matter-of-factly replied, "You know I never worked. Not even before we were married."

"But surely there was work involved in raising five children, and going to school to finish college, and keeping up the house," I said.

She looked a little confused. "But that wasn't work," she replied. "And as for the children, I wouldn't have traded that for anything. It never seemed like work to me."

"But of course it was work," I protested. But neither Ellie nor Michael pursued the matter, so we dropped it until the next morning when Ellie and I met and went for a walk.

"I haven't been able to get my mind off how I responded to your question last night," she said. "Of course I worked—*and I worked hard*—raising the children. In the early years of our marriage, we couldn't afford babysitters, and I remember months of caring for the children without a break."

"And when I went back to school, it was hard work. I forgot good study habits—if I ever had them!—and some courses were very difficult for me."

"The truth is that I still work hard taking care of the children, even though three of them are in high school and two are away in college. I also take care of the house and do entertaining for Michael. There are some days, still, when I'm totally exhausted."

"VENDIBLE COMMODITIES"

This exchange reveals how even intelligent people can believe work is measured in terms of product. Since almost all of the current literature, including many papal statements, defines work as something done outside the home and that involves pay, this attitude is not surprising.

Adam Smith addresses this line of thinking in his very influential work *Wealth of Nations*. Smith argues for work that produces some "particular subject" or "vendible commodity which lasts for some time at least after that labor is past." For Smith, work as economic activity creates wealth, makes possible the good life, and fosters civilization. Smith says human beings do not have to work in order to be human. But they must work to better their condition—a drive he holds as a distinguishing mark of being human.

Much of the work women have done and still do like carpooling, housekeeping, cooking, and child care, is considered unproductive in Smith's terms since it disappears even as it is being done. It is regarded as less important than work that yields a material product.

Mary Catherine Bateson confirms this in her book *Composing a Life*. She writes:

> Women are accustomed to tasks that have to be done again and again, tasks undone almost as soon as they are done. The dinner is eaten right after it is cooked, and there will be another dinner to think about tomorrow; the bed is unmade every night.

But she also challenges Smith and us to regard such activity as real work. It is for women to "compose" the creative contribution of their lives, Bateson says, "in scraps of rescued space and time, in marginal roles that have had to be invented again and again [where] the theme of improvisation is very clear."

In addition, a wage gap still exists between women and men. Though improved since the '70s, when women's rights activists wore buttons proclaiming "59¢" (out of every dollar), women and men still do not have the same earnings. In part this is due to the priority placed on market work versus family responsibilities. "Until family responsibilities are more equally shared," writes June O'Neill, the director of the Center for Business and Government at Baruch College, "women are not likely to have the same pattern of market work and earnings as men."

WORK THE SOUL NEEDS

The American novelist Alice Walker offers a touching reflection on the accomplishment of her own overworked mother

> who made all the clothes we wore, even my brothers'
> overalls. She made all the towels and sheets we used.
> She spent the summers canning vegetables and fruits.
> She spent the winter evenings making quilts enough
> to cover all our beds. During the 'working' day, she
> labored beside . . . my father in the fields. Her day
> began before sunup, and did not end until late at
> night.

Yet Walker's mother found time in the middle of all of these necessary demands to know and care about her own creative spirit.

That spirit was fed through the gardens surrounding the houses in which they lived—houses made beautiful by the bouquets of flowers she coaxed to bloom from early March to late November. Because of her mother's creativity with flowers, Walker writes, her memories of poverty are seen through a screen of blooms—sunflowers, petunias, roses, dahlias, forsythia, spiraea, delphinia.

Walker noticed that only when her mother worked with her flowers was she radiant, "almost to the point of being invisible—except as Creator: hand and eye. She was involved in work her soul needed to have."

How does the Christian define work? The Christian can offer a definition that includes more than paid labor. Learning is work. Caring for children is work. Volunteering is work. Community activism is work. Gardening is work. Thinking is work.

We also need to allow for work "that the soul must have"—creative and life-giving work. That might mean adjusting schedules so that a family member can serve as a volunteer firefighter while another becomes a student. Especially in financially strapped times, the unfortunate response to work "that the soul must have" is often an urging to work harder and longer at paying jobs: "If you've got so much extra time, why don't you sign up for overtime and earn some more money?" Or: "What do you mean you want to join the drama club? Why don't you try to squeeze in another class and get through college faster? Never mind enjoying it."

Comments like these bludgeon the human spirit. They deprive the soul and body of the release and freedom to come alive through the exercise of our gifts. Comments like these suffocate us.

SOULLESS WORK

Work should satisfy the needs of souls as well as bodies. After the thorough interviews he conducted for his book *Working*, Studs Terkel concluded that "most of us have jobs that are too small for our spirit."

E. F. Schumacher believes that soulless work is a tragedy. Too much of our concern, he believes, has been focused on how well the worker has been doing his or her job. Has she put in her assigned number of hours? Has he been diligent and efficient?

Schumacher believes we must look at the question the other way around and ask what work does to the worker. What kind of people have we become because of our work?

For work to benefit the worker, three conditions need to be present. First, work needs to be a means of self-expression. We need to be creatively engaged, bringing the best of our talents to bear on the task at hand. Second, the work needs to contribute to the relatedness of society. Serving others draws us out of ourselves. Third, work should serve a reconciling function. That reconciliation helps us see work not as something we must endure but as part of who we are. "I do not think I am exaggerating when I say that nine out of ten Christians feel that [a person's] work is always at the level of a 'spiritual encumbrance,'" wrote the working priest-paleontologist Pierre Teilhard de Chardin. Teilhard himself refused to lead a "double life" with work on one side and religious practice on the other. For Teilhard, these were not only reconcilable but a necessary expression of a faith that God is to be found in the world of matter if only we look.

Do What You Love and the Money Will Follow

Schumacher titles his book *Good Work*. Good work is possible when his three-step groundwork has been laid.

Good work is work suited to our gifts and talents. It is work we are good at, work where energy flows, work we are grateful to do. Often, people who find themselves in this situation say that they would do it for free.

Marsha Sinetar, the author of *Do What You Love and the Money Will Follow*, proposes that this kind of work is available to more people than we might think. Good work does not guarantee becoming financially wealthy, but it definitely is a source of spiritual wealth because we are fulfilled at the core of our beings.

Dr. Sinetar is not totally indifferent to the material benefits connected with work. She only wants to make the point that a bonanza of cash may not result—only, perhaps, enough money to get by. The greater benefit, however, comes from doing what we want to do.

While this plan of action seems to be outside the realm of possibility for many, she refuses to budge on her basic premise: Wouldn't it be desirable to go with the flow and follow one's dream with regard to one's work? Wouldn't it be attractive to wait it out until the "right" work came along and then jump on the wagon?

Desirable? Yes. Attractive? Yes. Practical? Not always. Sinetar is aware of the difficulty in pursuing this plan of action. Any of a hundred situations compromise the ideal. The responsibility (and work) of caring for sick parents, or a child or spouse; the wish not to uproot our children in the middle of their schooling; the limitations of geography; the forfeiture of retirement benefits and health insurance are just a few of the concerns that limit our options.

But she stands her ground. If the work we do is so unappealing, then the choices are simple: stick with it or find a better fit. If sacrifices need to be made, Sinetar has us believe they may be worth it. The tradeoff could be enjoyment rather than drudgery. Money or status that slips by in the bargain might not be worth complaint.

Sacrifice is a relative term. For the person engaged in work that is nonfulfilling and even destructive to the human spirit, the ultimate unhealthy sacrifice might be staying on the job.

Several years ago, my friends Carol and Will left their jobs in Boston and resettled in a small college town in Virginia. In their mid-forties, they had a now-or-never attitude about finally working at what they wanted to do. For Will, that meant opening his own computer consulting business. For Carol it meant illustrating children's books.

Their move involved uncertainty and risk. The first year did not bode well for the future: the local schools offered free computer consulting services, and Will could hardly compete with that. The poor economy affected publishing, and people who promised to give Carol assignments never did. But they waited it out, dug into their savings and drew closer in their marriage and their commitment to make a go of their plans.

At the beginning of the second year in Virginia, their daughter Carla was ready to enter college, but even the relatively modest fees connected with a state school were out of reach for the family. Carla postponed college and took on several part-time jobs to save money for the following year. She explained the situation to me this way:

> This move has made a big difference to Mom and Dad. Boston was a pressure cooker for them. Now they are so much more laid back. They enjoy things more. *They are around more.* If I had a choice between going to the college of my choice right now which would involve their doing something they didn't want to do to afford it—I'd choose this any day.

The decision "to do what you will" may be successful even when it does not look successful. "Modern civilization," on the other hand, as one observer wrote, "takes it for granted that people are better off the more things they want and are able to get; its values are quantitative and material. Now, 'How much is he worth?' means, 'How much has he got?'"

IMPERSONAL WORK

For those looking for spiritual satisfaction in their work, justice issues may surface such as just wages and worker alienation, with overcompensation and workaholism as new wrinkles in the area of depersonalization.

People must be paid a just wage in keeping with a standard of living that provides not only the bare necessities but also the time for leisure. It is possible (and sometimes necessary) to work one hundred hours each week to earn enough to support oneself and/or one's family. But that kind of commitment leaves very little time for personal recreation, which the spirit requires. This is true even when the spirit is nourished on the job, but especially so when it is not. The body also demands renewal time—time away from the factory, the office, the school, and the house in a different setting to allow the tensions to slide. A just wage means fair pay for a fair number of hours.

The typical chief executive officer of a major corporation in the United States earns roughly *160 times* what the average American worker earns, according to Graef S. Crystal, a business consultant and occasional professor at the University of California at Berkeley. This figure clearly shows the disparity between the working rich and the working poor, the lust for excess, and the insatiable appetite for competition in the United States. It may likewise explain why young people seek out courses of study, degrees, and majors that will potentially return the greatest dollar amount on their investment. And it may also explain why people put in such strenuous hours to earn more money until they reach the point of becoming workaholics. Plato knew that "poverty consists, not in the decrease of one's possessions, but in the increase of one's greed."

Whether or not its roots are in greed, workaholism is a disease in our culture as virulent in its effects as alcoholism and drug abuse, because it robs families of relationships and steals years of life from those afflicted.

WORK IS WHERE THEY GET THEIR KICKS

When it comes to discussing workaholism, we need to separate the workaholic from the person who simply and thoroughly enjoys his or her work.

Workaholics are compulsive. They work while they are at lunch, in the shower, on the plane, or at the dentist. They are often driven to perfectionism and are addicted to the high that working—and only working—brings. Work is where they get their kicks. Diane Fassel calls workaholism a killer disease. Marsha Sinetar and John Haughey also identify fear as one of the agents that drives the workaholic. Sinetar defines the workaholic as an "alienated, aggressive, stressed individual who typically uses work to stave off buried hostility, maladaptive social attitudes, and feelings of inadequacy." Haughey identifies the workaholic's fear as the need to avoid his or her own emptiness.

Healthy workers, on the other hand, may also be driven men and women, but their intention in working is "positive, loving, devotional, and earnestly sincere," according to Sinetar. Workaholics are so attached to their work that they *are* their work. Healthy workers separate themselves from their work and see their work as part but not all of who they are.

Workaholics tend to be competitive loners. The psychologist Jay Rohrlick claims that the workaholic's capacity for free choice is acutely limited. "An addiction is measured not by what an individual does, but by what he or she cannot do," Rohrlick says. "Only if a person cannot do *without* the excitement of work when such excitement is not appropriate or consciously desirable can we call him or her an addict. The work addict has no choice in the matter. . . . He cannot stop working."

Healthy workers are free to move away from their work. It does not constrict their development as human beings but rather expands it. Time away from work is welcomed as an occasion to relax and recharge batteries. It is a time to stretch and take personal inventory, with confidence that the responsibilities left behind will either be taken care of by other competent people or will remain undone with no critical side effects.

The only joy workaholics can envision is the satisfaction that work delivers and the buzz that keeps them going. Workaholics miss the splendor of sunsets and children growing up and the sorrows and joys of others. They are consumed by only one thing: work. They live for the rush that work gives them.

But only the individual can judge whether she or he is a workaholic. The symptoms may look the same to an outsider, but it would be unwise and unfair to assume that anyone who does not have time to share our personal preferences, passions, or company is a workaholic.

MONOTONY, REPETITION, AND ROUTINE

Worker alienation is another pathology connected with work. The German theologian Dorothee Soelle uses the image of the treadmill to capture the monotony of unsatisfying jobs and mindless duties.

If this is the "what" of alienation, there is no lack of clues concerning the "why." Some blame automation—the sense many workers have that they can be replaced by a machine or some other technology. Others turn to the restructuring of American business in which mergers and acquisitions are common and stability is jeopardized, to explain the powerlessness of the worker. Jobs that have us feel more like robots than humans, jobs that give us no opportunity to influence planning of our work, jobs in which only a few people see the completed product, and jobs that do not ask us to take initiatives—these all make us feel disconnected from our work.

The treadmill is a vivid image of mindless work. But for sheer power, the bare-bones description of worker alienation in prison offered by the Russian novelist Dostoevsky is unsurpassed.

If it were desired to crush and destroy a man completely and punish him with the most frightful possible penalty . . . it would suffice to give work the most completely and utterly useless and nonsensical character. Even though work is now dull and uninteresting for the convict, it is itself, as work, reasonable enough; the prisoner makes bricks, digs the soil, plasters walls, builds; there is purpose and an idea in such work. . . . But if he were compelled, for example, to pour water from one bucket into another and back into the first again . . . the prisoner, I think, would hang himself after a few days . . . choosing any way of escape, even death, from such degradation.

Dostoevsky's description leaves a few haunting questions in its wake. Are those condemned to live what he describes able to respond with anything other than despair? Is there some way to stare down this sense of uselessness and to emerge human and whole? Is there a way to effect the necessary change in the workplace so that alienation is lessened or even eliminated?

VALUING THE WORKER

The rift between workers and their work can be healed in a number of ways, starting with a change in attitude. We need to value work less and people more. In his encyclical letter *Laborem Exercens,* Pope John Paul II put it this way: "The basis for determining the value of human work is not primarily the kind of work being done, but the fact that the one who is doing it is a person."

This may be easier said than done. Our capitalist, profit-based economy is not structured to value the worker. Yet an attitude that favors labor over capital has benefits for the organization. The corporation known for its authentic, pro-people practices like generous vacations, parental leave, sabbaticals, college tuition for children, and child care can expect greater productivity, commitment, and loyalty from its employees, who know they are valued more for who they are than what they do.

THE FEELING OF BEING NEEDED ON EARTH

An openness that invites participation from everyone is also needed. "Sooner or later someone's going to catch the imagination of these people with some new magic. At the bottom of it will be a promise of regaining the feeling of participation, the feeling of being needed on earth—hell, *dignity*." These words come from the American novelist Kurt Vonnegut, describing people without access to meaningful work. And he is right on target.

If we are serious about counteracting worker alienation, we need to allow workers to participate more fully in policy, decision making, and the product itself (when one exists). The pretense that participatory management and servant leadership exist, when in truth they do not, is demoralizing. The climate of the organization is seriously eroded when workers detect hypocrisy in mission statements that call for the contribution of a diverse team and then settle on the counsel of only a select, predetermined few who turn out to be clones of those in charge.

Not many major organizations offer strong leadership concerning participation and diversity in the workplace. But certainly the Xerox Corporation is one that does. Because of one of the most assertive affirmative action and diversity programs in the nation, 17% of Xerox's vice-presidents and directors are minorities—and the number is on the rise. The national average for minorities in management teeters between 7 and 9 percent.

Xerox's program has been effective because the company assures that minority employees get the experience and training they need to move up the ladder and through the glass ceiling. But Xerox has also used tactics considered radical just a few years ago, like encouraging minority caucus groups and national "networks" providing support and advice to African-American employees—and later, female, Asian, and Hispanic employees. Xerox is consciously aware that during this decade, 80 percent of new people entering the marketplace as workers will be minority groups or women. This requires a serious rethinking of conventional employment patterns of the past. At Xerox, the goal is to give all employees, but especially minorities, freedom to participate in the company full-tilt and to advance themselves.

Other companies are copying Xerox. In the meantime, step by step, Xerox models the style that reinforces the dignity of the corporation and its workers. *All workers.*

PRIDE IN QUALITY

Pride in one's work is an antidote to worker alienation. This attitude is considerably easier to elicit when the other attitudes are in place—those that value the person and allow participation, which in turn enable workers to see the whole picture. The story of three men breaking rocks makes this point.

"What are you doing?" a passerby asks.

"Making little rocks out of big ones," says the first worker.

"Earning a living," answers the second.

"Building a cathedral," says the third.

All of the answers are correct, but the last one reflects pride in one's work and the ability to see through a task to the humanizing joint venture and mission at hand.

An attitude of pride in one's work—whatever one is doing—produces quality in the long run. Work needs focus and attention to the aesthetic dimension, building the cathedral, but we cannot build a cathedral without breaking rocks.

We need an attitude toward our work that inspires us. And we need to build a cathedral. Or a family. Or a better world.

WORK AND CONTEMPLATION

Contemplation is crucial to work. Work without contemplation diminishes us because contemplation asks us to step back from what we are doing, making, and planning to wonder about our relationship to it.

Once, an author friend of mine handed me the draft of a completed manuscript. "Tell me," he said, "whether publishing this book is worth destroying a small forest of trees." He had obviously contemplated the network of relationships, which involved death (the trees) and life (the book), weighed its impact, and asked me to do likewise.

Contemplation does that. It points to respect for people, whales, children, arteries, rivers, as well as trees and books.

Contemplation also invites us to question whether our work is complementary with God's vision for the universe. The vision in the background is always *leiturgia* or liturgy, "the work of the people," which breathes life into the work of human hands, blesses it, and makes it the sign or sacrament of the very holiness of God. Liturgy gathers a community that insists on right order, right relationships— on solidarity that erases lines of division between management and labor, profits and losses, minority and majority hiring, glass ceilings and quotas, layoffs and promotions. Liturgy claims dignity for God's children and the right to work for all.

Until the liturgy is reflected in factories, offices, and relationships all over the world, our work and our mission will be out of kilter with the ideal.

TO EXERCISE WORK

How does one exercise the privilege of working? How do we find fulfillment in work?

1. *Work with another person or several persons on a project*. Teamwork speaks of the capacity of the human heart to depend on others and to share and to build a better world *together*. This is a particularly fruitful way of working because it allows for community to exist.

2. *Share the unpleasant tasks.* Find ways to take turns with the less popular parts of a job. For example, if the work involves being present on holidays, look for ways to share the burden of being away from families and friends so that the responsibility does not always fall on the same person. There may be people who have a high tolerance for certain unpleasant tasks. Express the gratitude of the entire team when someone willingly takes over such responsibility for a long time.

3. *Find something you love doing and do it.* Work at something that gives *you* pleasure. Even if this is not the source of your full-time employment, decide that you owe it to yourself to be involved in some effort that is joyful.

4. *Volunteer.* Not every valuable job needs to have a price tag attached. When a paycheck is absent, the gift of ourselves is more accurately just that—self-donation.

The poor tend to make the greatest contributions to charity. As a group, people in the United States with household incomes of less than $10,000 a year give the highest percentage of their income and time to charitable causes. The richest give the least.

5. *Look for diversity in the workplace.* Choose to work for a company or institution that goes out of its way to hire a mixed work force. Look for racial, religious, and cultural diversity. And do what you can to make all people feel at home. If a hearing-impaired worker spends her lunchtime eating alone or reading a book, consider proposing a course in signing for everyone to encourage communication. Breaking down barriers is often effected best through simple but sincere person-to-person gestures.

6. *If you are in a position to reward someone, consider incentives other than money.* Most employees say they would rather have time than money, anyway. A day off, especially around the holidays, is often a great bonus. Think about offering employees a weekend away as a bonus. Offer time at a retreat center, or a cabin at the beach or in the mountains. Be creative.

7. *Quality matters.* Strive for it in everything. Expect it in work done for you and in products you purchase. Demand it of yourself.

8. *Teach children that all facets of a job matter and need to be done well.* Kevin Walsh, a professor of education at the University of Alabama, says that what is wrong with America's schools is that children paint beautiful pictures but do not clean their paintbrushes. When a child is asked to take care of the class rabbit, he or she is delighted to do so but avoids cleaning the cage. If children are equipped to exercise self-discipline, they will develop character and self-esteem. "The development of character is the backbone of the economic system," Professor Walsh says. "It is the fiber by which the work ethic develops."

9. *Learn about groups that link work and spirituality.* The National Center for the Laity, headquartered in Chicago, is one of them. This team of men and women who work also prepare creative resources for people who work—all kinds of people: firefighters, carpenters, accountants, salespeople, politicians, electricians, administrators, and many others. Their insights are empowering.

10. *Treasure the sabbath. It was made for rest and leisure.* This is easy to forget with 24-hour malls and supermarkets and so much work to do around the house. The Sabbath puts a brake on labor, profits, productivity, and competition, and opens the heart to a contemplative way of relating to work—and to everything else.

11. *Thank people who do work for you.* The mailperson, your children's teachers, the baggers at the grocer's, the pharmacist, the reservations clerk, secretaries, baby-sitters, barbers, and hairdressers. Think of creative ways to express gratitude rather than just giving money.

12. *Nurture the contemplative side of your work.* Give yourself the time to reflect on what kind of person you've become because of your work. How does what you do and how you do it contribute to God's vision for the universe?

In one of his interviews for *Working,* Studs Terkel interviewed Nora Watson, who believes that "most of us are looking for a calling, not a job." The Bible calls it a mission—the kind God wants us to share.

When we nurture the contemplative side of our work, we raise the stakes about what we do and for whom we do it. Real satisfaction in work lies in our mission with God.

NOTES

The epigraph comes from *Working* by Studs Terkel (New York: Pantheon Books, 1972), xxiv.

The Ben & Jerry information comes from an article by Kathryn Larrabee, "Ben Cohen Runs a Business with a Mission," in *Business Insurance,* a publication of Crain Communications (Chicago), April 22, 1991, T27; and a brief story in the *Wall Street Journal,* April 23, 1991, C12(E). Another story, "Just Desserts," by Robert E. Sullivan, Jr., appearing in *Rolling Stone,* July 9–23, 1992, 75–79, was consulted.

For the understanding of Genesis, I depended largely on Francis Fiorenza. See his "Work and Critical Theology," in *A Matter of Dignity,* edited by W. J. Heisler and John W. Houck (Notre Dame, IN: University of Notre Dame Press, 1977), 23–44. This article is an excellent contribution to a fine collection by Heisler and Houck.

The comments on the productivity of God in Genesis by John Haughey are to be found in his book *Converting Nine to Five: A Spirituality of Daily Work* (New York: Crossroad, 1989), 31–37; his comments on worker alienation cited later in my text can be found in his book, 29–31.

James Weldon Johnson's poem "The Creation" is found in *God's Trombones: Seven Negro Sermons in Verse* (New York: Penguin Books, 1981, reprint of the 1969 edition), 17–20.

E. F. Schumacher, *Good Work* (New York: Harper & Row, 1979), delineates the conditions for good work on 3–4.

The definition of work from Miroslav Volf comes from *Work in the Spirit: Toward a Theology of Work* (New York: Oxford University Press, 1991), 7.

The reference to "vendible commodity" comes from Adam Smith, *Wealth of Nations* (New York: The Modern Library, 1937), 314. Smith singled out work as virtually the only source of economic wealth and placed it at the heart of economic theory. See P. J. McNulty, "Adam

Smith's Concept of Labour," in the *Journal of the History of Ideas* 34 (1973), 345–366.

See Mary Catherine Bateson, *Composing a Life* (New York: Penguin Books/Plume, 1990), 213, for the remarks on the ephemeral nature of woman's work. The quotation on improvisation is found on 11.

June O'Neill's survey of the progress in closing the wage gap can be found in "Women and Wages: Gender Pay Ratios/The American Enterprise," *Current* 331 (March/April 1991), 10–16.

Alice Walker is quoted from "In Search of Our Mothers' Gardens," in *In Search of Our Mothers' Gardens* (San Diego: Harcourt Brace Jovanovich, 1984), 231–243. For the quotations, see 238, 241.

Pierre Teilhard de Chardin's observation about the double life is located in *The Divine Milieu* (New York: Harper & Bros., 1960), 34.

Marsha Sinetar, *Do What You Love and the Money Will Follow* (New York: Bantam Dell, 1987), is the source of information about doing what we want to do. See especially 1–16 and 109–125.

A. K. Coomaraswamy is the source of the quotation about modern civilization and quantitative values. See *The Bugbear of Literacy* (London: Dennis Dobson, 1943), 2.

Graef S. Crystal's study of how and what U.S. executives are paid is titled *In Search of Excess: The Overcompensation of American Executives* (New York: Norton, 1991).

For Plato on poverty and greed, see his dialogue *Laws,* Ch. 5 (736) in *The Dialogues of Plato,* translated by B. Jowett (New York: Random House, 1937), 503.

On the issue of workaholism, see Marsha Sinetar, cited earlier, 148 ff.; John C. Haughey, S.J., cited earlier, 91–94; and Anne Wilson Schaef and Diane Fassel, *The Addictive Organization* (San Francisco: Harper & Row, 1988), 129–136. In a separate very fine book, *Working Ourselves to Death* (San Francisco: HarperSanFrancisco, 1990), Diane Fassel speaks of workaholism as a killer disease.

Another source on workaholism is Jay Rohrlick, *Work and Love* (New York: Summit Books, 1960), 165–166.

Dorothee Soelle with Shirley A. Cloyes, *To Work and to Love* (Philadelphia: Fortress Press, 1984), also comment on worker alienation.

F. M. Dostoevsky, *Memoirs from the House of the Dead,* translated by Jessie Coulson (London: Oxford University Press, 1965), 24, is the source of the quotation about mindless work.

See John Paul II, *On Human Work* (*Laborem Exercens*), in *Origins* 11 (September 24, 1981), for his comments on the dignity of the worker.

Kurt Vonnegut, *Piano Player* (New York: Avon Books, 1952), 94, also comments on dignity and the worker.

For information on the Xerox Corporation, I consulted "A New Push to Break the Glass Ceiling," by Leon E. Wynter and Jolie Solomon, in the *Wall Street Journal*, November 15, 1989: B1. "Race in the Workplace," the cover story in *Business Week*, July 8, 1991, 50–63, and the transcript of the segment on Xerox on The MacNeil-Lehrer NewsHour, October 29, 1991, were also very helpful.

Richard Leucke's article "Work and Contemplation," is part of a festschrift for Douglas and Dorothy Steere entitled *Spirituality in Ecumenical Perspective,* forthcoming from Westminster Press. Both Leucke and Douglas Steere informed my comments on liturgy, contemplation, and work.

Eric N. Berg reported on Kevin Walsh's experiments in values education in "Argument Grows That Teaching of Values Should Rank with Lessons," *The New York Times* (National Edition), January 1, 1992, 36.

Studs Terkel quotes Nora Watson on work as a calling in *Working,* cited earlier, xxiv.

Chapter 5

Weeping

Do grown men weep? Sure. Should grown men weep?
Of course. Anyone in touch with reality in this world
knows there are lots of reasons to weep.
Max DePree, *Leadership Is an Art*

Eang Long is blind. Her vision began to fade on the day when she was rounded up by the Khmer Rouge along with her brother, his wife, and their three children. The adults were forced to witness as the soldiers clubbed the two older children to death. Then Long's brother and sister-in-law were killed. Finally, a soldier lifted the last child, an infant, by the leg and smashed him to death against a tree.

Eang Long has been blind since then.

Chhean Im, another refugee from the killing fields of Cambodia, is also blind. Her father and brother were killed before her eyes. The last thing she remembers seeing was a particularly savage killing. "I started crying hard for a long time. It felt like there was a big needle pushing through my head." Days later, when Chhean Im stopped crying, she could not see.

Though both women are blind, there is nothing clinically wrong with their vision. Both have been examined by Gretchen Van Boemel, the associate director of clinical electrophysiology at the Doheny Eye

Institute in Los Angeles. Van Boemel and other scientists are convinced that to escape from trauma, the women sacrificed their sight and are now psychosomatically blind.

In simple but tragic terms, they cried until they could not see. Though the power of tears may have taken their sight, it may also have preserved their sanity.

Another Cambodian refugee, Arn Chorn, believes tears can change human madness into love. An 18-year-old survivor of the Khmer Rouge, Arn told the annual general meeting of Amnesty International USA in 1988 of the power of tears:

> I am not ashamed to cry. All of us need not be ashamed to cry. In fact, maybe the first thing we have to do is cry. Our tears may even be the power necessary to change violence into love—change human madness to human kindness. The tears may be the water of new life.
>
> So I offer you the tears of all Cambodian children who have suffered so much, and we join with the tears of all those who suffer yesterday and today, and we cry with you, "Please, never again. No more Cambodian genocide, no more Jewish holocausts, no more Beirut massacres, no more El Salvadors."

THE STIGMA OF WEEPING

In our culture, weeping suffers from an image problem. It makes us appear weak, whiny, or passive. And yet it is vital that we weep, both for ourselves and others.

Weeping engages us in the grief and misfortune of someone else, where we recognize suffering as the basis of our common humanity. This is its raw potential—to connect us with each other. To decline to weep with another is to settle for being less than human. Weeping unleashes a baptism of tears that energizes us for action and moves us toward eradicating the roots of injustice.

The weeping I am advocating, however, does not function only on the emotional level; it involves an intellectual commitment as well. It is the one-two punch of both the heart and mind that best serves to raise consciousness about some unfairness, injustice, or evil that simply can no longer be tolerated among rational and civilized, let alone Christian, people.

BUFFERED AGAINST SUFFERING

Sometimes we decline to make that commitment to weep for another. A bewildered friend of mine sent me this note on her Christmas card this year: "My address will probably change in the next few weeks. I am paying an outrageous rent to live on the 32nd floor of a luxury apartment building on the East Side of Manhattan while four homeless men sleep over the building's heating grates on the street below me. The city can't cope. I can't cope. It's very depressing. So I am going to move where these men are not the first things I see every morning and the last things I see every night."

But where will she go to escape suffering? There is no such place.

The ideal life proposed for us by our culture is one free from suffering, or at least buffered against its sting, and we have enough medication and excuses to avoid pain most of the time. Suffering embarrasses us; a suffering Savior is still scandalous to many. In the face of embarrassment and scandal, it is easy to be tempted to keep one's distance.

A colleague recently told me how uncomfortable he felt calling a mutual friend after the death of her mother. "What will I say?" he wondered. He solved his dilemma, as millions do, by purchasing a sympathy card. A lovely photograph of a sunset on the cover of the card glowed in oranges and blues. Printed inside, the text read, "Sending comforting thoughts your way." The tone was antiseptic and appropriate to send if the friend broke an ankle or a crystal vase. And that might have been part of its appeal—it wasn't too personal. He didn't send the card. Instead, he fumbled but found his own words.

THE ILLUSION OF PAINLESSNESS

To weep is countercultural. It opposes numbness, apathy, and indifference and invites us to get involved. It urges us not to betray or abandon those who are afflicted but asks that we articulate their pain by weeping, as the Psalmist did centuries ago, sometimes in rage, sometimes through screams, sometimes through silent tears. The German theologian Dorothee Soelle is convinced that only those who are able to weep with another will work to abolish conditions where people are exposed to unnecessary suffering such as hunger, oppression, or torture. "The ideal of a life free from suffering" and "the illusion of painlessness," she writes, "destroys people's ability to feel anything."

But if painlessness is an illusion, it is an illusion many of us would like to sustain. Our practiced efforts at keeping pain at bay and at not allowing others or ourselves to experience suffering has, ironically, reached epidemic proportions. We excel at "spin control," which allows us to pretend that suffering does not exist, and when it is undeniable, we prefer to eliminate the sufferer rather than to face the cause of the suffering. And in the process, we have domesticated suffering—contained it, if not erased it—and we have erased some of our common humanity in the bargain.

THE COLLECTIVE SOB

Philosopher Stanley Hauerwas claims that suffering makes the other a stranger. Since suffering tends to distance us from each other, our first reaction is to be repelled by it. "Suffering makes people's otherness stand out in strong relief," he writes, "but that otherness is exactly the condition to force recognition of them and ourselves." In other words, when we weep with another, we are connected to a common humanity that breaks down walls of division and claims our relationship to each other as brothers and sisters. Weeping gives us access to that collective sob and the hurts of all men and women.

The poem "Common Life" shows how this collective sob unites us all:

> *Waiting for a lab report,*
> *Dependent on mysterious authorities,*
> *Gazing at my daughter in hospital,*
> *Her mother and I sharing a hard fellowship,*
> *I know a timeless, tribeless circumstance:*
> *I drive to the hospital in an eternal procession,*
> *I eat in the snack bar among the whole human race;*
> *My tears began 100,000 years ago*
> *And will never stop.*

The depth of this connection allows us to walk in another's shoes and to live in another's skin at least for a while. Allowing ourselves to weep, and others to weep, is the beginning of the discovery of who we are.

My own most vivid recollection of living in the skin of someone else happened in grade school and high school, when I became physically ill reading of the gas ovens at Dachau, Auschwitz, and elsewhere. As the Christian daughter of a Jewish father, I shared the legacy of Judaism at close range in a family with relatives named Rebecca, Aaron, Ruth, Joel, and David. Yet as much as I was shaken by the obscenities of Nazi cruelty—and I was shaken to the core—I was also impressed with the goodness of people like Raoul Wallenberg, Corrie ten Boom, and Andre Trocmé, who defied the Hitler regime. Imagine risking imprisonment to shelter Jews, as the ten Boom family did in the Netherlands! Anne Frank and Etty Hillesum entreated us not to forget what happened but to transcend it. In the long run their heroism and dignity outweighed the malevolence of their oppressors.

Anne Frank and Etty Hillesum are members of a long chain of people who were both powerless in their suffering and powerful in their capacity to weep for others. They are the contemporary version of prophets of the Old Testament who refused to be silenced by the dominant corrupt political consciousness. Their response, while passionate, was never violent. Violence would have turned their rage into hatred and destroyed them in the process.

Lesser known people have done the same. Felicia Bernstein ingeniously organized women of the world during the Vietnam War of the sixties in a campaign under a banner declaring that "War is not healthy for children and other living things." Jean Vanier worked among the mentally handicapped and gathered a first group of such people together in Trosly, France, and taught them to speak and to make steps toward independence while safely surrounded by love.

Like Jeremiah and Jesus before them, these men and women entered into the sorrow of others daily. The vanquished, the humiliated, and the banished matter because their hurt matters. Injury, violence, and loss are given a voice, and a public voice is absolutely critical if change is to occur. Walter Brueggemann sizes up the wisdom of the strategy this way: "Bringing hurt to public expression is an important first step in the criticism that makes clear that things are not as they should be, not as they were promised, and not as they will and must be."

Do Not Suffer Without Complaining

"Do not suffer without complaining"—those are eloquent words. And they demand that we recognize that the opposite is often the case. When we hide our hurt and resign ourselves to it, we succumb to it. Learning to suffer without complaining is bad advice. We must acknowledge that we have been wronged, or that someone else has been mistreated, or simply that we are in pain. That is the beginning of change—in attitudes, in funding for research against disease, in the alteration of foreign policy. Speaking out operates on the extraordinary assumption that someone will listen. The ultimate listener, of course, is a just God, but the amazing thing is that this just God has friends among us who respond to the voice of conscience once the truth is spoken.

"BLESSED ARE YOU WHO WEEP NOW" (LUKE 6:21)

What characteristics distinguish people who weep?

People who weep with other people allow themselves to be affected by human misery and are capable of reaching down into a deep reservoir of compassion so that they really do *feel with another.* Not content merely to sympathize with another's pain, these men and women also know how *to take action,* or how to get other people *to do the same,* or how to get the victims *to stand in defense of themselves,* and usually, how *to be with the victims* while the doing gets done.

Weeping with the suffering also mobilizes us to help. We must be willing to get our hands dirty—to participate with the suffering, not merely as onlookers full of suggestions.

Those who weep with others usually put their bodies as well as their spirits on the line, like Habitat for Humanity, the outreach program that builds low-income homes or rejuvenates blighted ones. Or the shelters for abused women or homeless persons, or the detoxification centers that also house people who see the urgent value of the work being done and are there to be of help.

RISKING CONFLICT WITH THE POWERFUL

People who weep with other people are unafraid of conflict. They may find conflict unpleasant, but they do not withdraw from it. Nor do they cave in to despair or pessimism when the conflict gets rough. They freely relinquish the desire to win popularity contests when they sign on with unpopular causes. And they are able to see the creative possibilities of working through conflict to new solutions.

To espouse the cause of the powerless is always to risk conflict with the powerful. This is precisely why the powerless need someone to feel their pain and to weep with them.

Apathy is a voice that says, "What can you do? There's misery all around and you've got to live with it." But people who weep with other people see the possibilities in change. They refuse to put up with gratuitous suffering when a regulation can be altered or a building can be renovated. Those who weep with others see change as an essential human value and do not flinch at conflict to alter the unjust status quo.

Oscar Romero, the archbishop of El Salvador, did not flinch. He wept with and for his people and he indicted their oppressors. The gentle archbishop called things as he saw them: he called parts of the government corrupt, he urged conversion, he invited repentance. When he read the riot act, everyone knew who the rioters were. He spoke the truth until he was silenced in a hospital chapel, gunned down as he was celebrating the Eucharist on April 2, 1980.

Though his voice is gone, others have taken up the cause of the poor and marginalized in Central America. Others weep with them now. And those who thought they could silence the truth ironically attached loudspeakers to it for all the world to hear and weep for the cause that claimed the life of this holy man.

THOSE WHO WEEP ARE NOT LONERS

People who weep with other people know the value of community. They are not loners. They attract followers and galvanize movements. The civil rights leaders did this in the '60s: they spoke out clearly against racial bigotry and claimed that the time had come to march toward fuller equality for all citizens of our country.

Plowshares, SANE-FREEZE, Pax Christi, Ground Zero, and other groups protesting the nuclear stockpiling also depend on numbers, and the quality of their membership, for their strength and the durability of their message. Their message is simple enough: there are already three tons of TNT for every man, woman, and child in the world. Do we really need to stockpile any more? And is it really fair to divert monies to this cause when the poor are still with us?

As long ago as the third century, Saint Basil of Caesarea asked the same questions this way: "How can I make you realize the misery of the poor? How can I make you understand that your wealth comes from their weeping?"

RE-IMAGING THE FUTURE

People who weep with other people are men and women of hope. Hope does not deny the severity of the pain or the depth of the grief. Hope does not wash away the brutality of the torture or the near-madness suffered by the victims.

What hope does, after the grief is experienced, after the pain breaks us in two, and after more tears than we thought possible are shed, is to refuse sorrow's logical routing into despair. The power of the mother of Jesus at the foot of the cross or in Michelangelo's rendition of the Pietà is that she does not yield to anger, hopelessness, or depression. Her ultimate attraction to us is that she clings to a hope, even after all her dreams and those of her son seem shattered. In hope, she is able to re-image the future. In hope, she is able to say that a future is possible.

"GOD'S HEART WAS THE FIRST TO BREAK"

Why do good people suffer?

Why does a good God allow suffering?

I do not know the answers to these questions, but I have learned from the sufferings of others three very important truths about God: God weeps, Jesus suffered, and suffering did not defeat Jesus. Nor does it defeat those who believe in him.

God weeps with victims of injustice and speaks on their behalf. The God that Isaiah depicts when he asks, "Can a woman forget her nursing child, or show no compassion for the child of her womb?" (Isa. 49:15) is a God who passionately participates in the lives of her people—a God who plays, weeps, laughs, enjoys. Jesus, too, wept. He wept over Jerusalem, he wept when he heard his friend Lazarus had died, and in Gethsemane he was sorrowful even unto death.

This is the Savior in whom we believe: one who hears and identifies with the cries of the poor so directly that he tells us that when we do something for one of the neglected and abused ones, we, in fact, befriend Christ himself (Matt. 25). Or, to put it the way theologian Matthew Lamb does: "The cries of the victims . . . are the voice of the living God." It's as simple, and as awesome, as that.

The identification of God with suffering humankind is so complete that Elie Wiesel can write and rivet us with this account:

> The SS hung two Jewish men and a boy before the assembled inhabitants of the camp. The men died quickly but the death struggle of the boy lasted half an hour. "Where is God? Where is he?" a man behind me asked. As the boy, after a long time, was still in agony on the rope, I heard the man cry again, "Where is God now?" And I heard a voice within me answer, "Here he is—he is hanging here on this gallows."

Where is God when someone suffers? God is there with that person, raging, weeping, suffering. Protestant pastor and social activist William Sloane Coffin ratifies the undeniable solidarity between God and the victim:

> As almost all of you know, a week ago last Monday night, driving in a terrible storm . . . my twenty-four-year-old Alexander, who enjoyed beating his old man at every game and in every race, beat his father to the grave.
>
> When a person dies, there are many things that can be said, and there is at least one thing that should never be said. . . . The one thing that should never be said when someone dies is, "It is the will of God. " Never do we know enough to say that.
>
> My own consolation lies in knowing that it was *not* the will of God that Alex die; that when the waves closed over the sinking car, God's heart was the first of all our hearts to break.

But we know something else as well about God. God sent a first-born son who lived among us and suffered a cruel death. The record states that Jesus was unjustly accused, that he endured a rigged trial, torture, and a criminal's execution. Death by crucifixion is clinically a death by suffocation: enough blood cannot be pumped to the heart—enough air cannot reach the lungs. The body of the victim heaves in violent spasms before expiring.

Jesus also suffered emotionally and psychologically. Peter denied knowing him, Judas traded him in for money, his friends fled at the last hour, and he felt abandoned by God and a profound sense of amputation from his roots.

THE GOD OF POWER IS THE GOD WHO WEEPS

The Japanese Christian writer Shusaku Endo in his novel *Silence* provides unusual depth of understanding on the subject of God's suffering with us. The theme of the book focuses on the shifting image of God and self in the life of a dedicated young Jesuit missionary in seventeenth-century Japan.

The God who initially inspires Father Rodrigues is a God of power and might, a Christ of glory, a victorious Jesus who demands heroism from his disciples and even martyrdom during this time of persecution in Japan. Clearly this is a God of the strong who judges with severity and casts aside the lukewarm and the weak.

But the God who Father Rodrigues meets in Japan is not an exalted but a kenotic (or emptying) God who identifies with those for whom he has suffered. It is the God of the *fumie* (the bronze plaque with the face of Jesus upon which Christians were obliged to trample while renouncing their faith)—weak, powerless, anguished, emaciated. The Christ of the *fumie,* unlike the triumphal God, has compassion for the betrayer and knows well the pain in the foot of the apostate who tramples upon his face.

The spiritual journey of Father Rodrigues, deftly narrated by Endo, begins with a romanticized vision of his own mission and the heroic martyrdom he anticipates. It ends with a revelation of the true face of the Christ—sunken, exhausted, compassionate, and forgiving.

All of the efforts of early Christianity to hide the sufferings of Jesus seem to miss the point that it is only a suffering Messiah like the Christ of the *fumie* who could be intelligible to us. It is only a weeping

Messiah who would understand the depth of our sorrow and our tears. Only a co-suffering Savior, rather than one of power and might, could reveal power in his powerlessness and fullness in his emptiness.

That fullness is revealed in ways impossible for one without faith to accept. The broken body of Jesus is restored to wholeness. The darkness of Good Friday yields to the light of a resurrection on Easter. The indestructible power of love forces us to put the power of evil and hatred in perspective. But the resurrected Jesus does not forget the world in turmoil and the suffering human community. In paradise, the gaze of Jesus is not directed upward but downward. It is directed at us and perhaps most particularly where suffering is a widely distributed experience—where every man, woman, and not infrequently many a child is directly confronted with evil itself.

It is then that the life and death of Jesus is put to the acid test. Does it make a difference if the sufferer has faith? Yes, it does.

Russian philosopher Nicholas Berdayaev is on to something of supreme importance when he suggests a paradox associated with suffering—namely, that both good and evil can flow from it. It is the peculiar insight of the Christian, however, to see the possibility of love as pointing to a victory, to choose the good and to redeem suffering. It is then that tears can be wiped away.

CAN GOOD COME FROM SUFFERING?

The idea that suffering can be redeemed is made concrete in the spellbinding account of the torture and prison experience of Iulia de Beausobre in Russia in the 1930s during the Stalinist purge. Ms. de Beausobre endured solitary confinement for three months, followed by imprisonment in the deepest recesses of solitary called the "Inner" for another three months. Since most people cracked in less than six weeks with their nerves irrevocably destroyed, Ms. de Beausobre's endurance was regarded as remarkable. Used as a guinea pig in medical experimentation after her interrogation was over, she was then sentenced to five years of hard labor.

Ms. de Beausobre lived to tell her story. And God's. She found it possible to derive good from suffering.

When confronted with sadistic people who delighted in torturing her, Ms. de Beausobre learned that there is only one way to make your torturers stop tormenting you, and that is to become invulnerable. Cease to be interesting to your torturer and you will eventually be left alone.

There are two ways to achieve this end. One route is passivity, surrender to a "clodlike, indifferent, subhuman" existence. The other way is supremely active, to take everything in and attempt to penetrate the mind of the captor. "All this is very hard," Ms. de Beausobre writes. "Once it is achieved, you realize that you have been privileged to take part in nothing less than an act of redemption. And then you find that, incidentally and inevitably, you have reached a form of serenity which is, if anything, more potent to counteract sadistic lusts than any barren impassivity could be."

The serenity of which Ms. de Beausobre speaks is connected with feeling and knowing beyond all possible doubt that "notwithstanding all the tormentors' devices, there is, and always will remain, within you something that is built on rock. . . . Being both of you and of the rock . . . it cannot be uprooted. Besides, being of eternity, the more it is laid bare the brighter it shines."

Ms. de Beausobre shows that the fortitude of the tortured is very different when they think of themselves only as poor, lonely wretches and when they think of themselves as members of the mystical body of Christ. Only the latter are likely to come through without succumbing to hatred. Moreover, it is only they who can pool their terrible experiences with the redemptive work of others. They alone can raise their harrowing experience from the level of a personal evil, or even of a personal matter at all, and make of it an impersonal enrichment, a universal good, a part of the redemptive work of Christ in his mystical body—the Church.

The cup of suffering becomes the cup of strength. Passed from one of us to the other, it empowers us to weep with our brothers and sisters, present and past, across the globe.

BENEFITS OF WEEPING

Three benefits of weeping eclipse all others.

Jeremiah in the Old Testament and Peter in the New show us that weeping keeps us real and vulnerable to the human condition. Jeremiah wept for Judah before anyone else because he realized that Judah and its people would be destroyed. Jeremiah's personal love for his country and its people conflicted and wrenched his heart. He knew the accuracy of the prophecy—he knew the end was coming and that the freedom of God had been grossly violated. But his spirit grieved over the news that he had to deliver and so he wept. He wept because he was made of flesh and blood.

Peter wept because he confronted his own weakness and saw it for what it was (see Luke 22:62). The fledgling Christian community expected strength of its new leader, but Peter was a mixed bag of insecurity, fear, and brashness. When he was called on to pledge his allegiance to his Master, he reneged and denied him three times. And then regretted his cowardice and wept.

In his wisdom, Jesus had entrusted the power to forgive sins to the one apostle, on record at least, who wept for his sins (Matt. 16:19). Maybe it was Peter's understanding of the human condition and its need for mercy and unconditional reconciliation that qualified him in his Master's eyes for the honor of holding in trust the keys of the kingdom. Arrogance and domination are inconsistent if mercy falls unrestrained like gentle dew from the heavens. Peter's gift of tears guarantees the gentle touch of one who understands the treason and hypocrisy that lurk in the human heart.

The second benefit of weeping is the gift of friendship. Tears bond us to those who are defenseless, weak, and cast aside. The collective sob unites us to all who have suffered and allows us to claim them as friends. And those who weep with us and our sufferings—the losses in our lives, the limitations of health, the unfinished dreams—promise us that we will never be alone.

We know for certain that Jesus had friends and two of them, Mary and Martha, revealed their loss to him. Lazarus died, and the bonds of friendship were tender enough to elicit the tears of Jesus and strong enough to resurrect Lazarus from death (John 11:1-44). Such is the power of one who understands the language of weeping.

The third benefit of weeping is the return we receive on our investment of giving to others. The expression most often used by Jesus goes something like this: "The one who holds on to life, loses it, but the one who lets go, gains life" (see John 12:25). The teaching of Jesus is a fundamental paradox: that to exist, you must give yourself away.

This is not a command; it is a description. Giving oneself away—especially through tears for another—is not what "ought" to be done but what self-giving really means. Love is the ground of all existence. Being and loving are synonymous. If you exist at any rich level of being at all, you must give yourself away.

Life and death are paradigms for the giving away of self and so is the Eucharist: Jesus is the One who is consumed so that others can be nourished. We, in turn, are asked to become "eucharist" so that others may live.

The proposition is simple: If you want to live, give yourself away. If you want to live forever, then give yourself away totally. When Jesus gave himself away to his sisters and brothers, and to the One he called Father, the tomb could not hold him. He died but could not stay dead.

Weeping with others—emptying ourselves to enter the pain of another—gives us privileged access to this everlasting life.

TO EXERCISE WEEPING

Weeping exercises the eyes. So we need to begin with where we look and what our eyes see.

1. *Look for places where there is pain and offer to share it.* This is a gesture of friendship where some kindness might be welcome—transportation to a doctor, baby-sitting, a home-cooked dinner, or simple presence. This exercise calls for sharing pain, not relieving it, so

share unobtrusively and respectfully. Sometimes, we share by simply telling another person that we are available.

2. *Look for places where injustices exist and get involved.* There are churches across the country that are providing sanctuary for Central American, Haitian, and other refugees. There are parish congregations running soup kitchens, food pantries, shelters, day care centers, and tutoring services, and almost all of them need dependable volunteers. The kingdom of God is built on earth not by spectacular leaps but small steps. One night a week. Or one afternoon. It will make a difference.

3. *Read the newspaper.* Or better still, read two. Read magazines and books and whatever else you can get your hands on.

Weigh the facts. Let the reading lead you to question the status quo. Let one story lead you to another story . . . and another. Become informed in some depth about an issue—apartheid, child abuse, death squads, capital punishment. All of these invite participation and our tears for the cause of justice.

4. *Try on a new pair of glasses.* See the world from a different point of view. A new pair of glasses, figuratively speaking, helps. Try looking at a trip to the supermarket from the vantage point of senior citizens on fixed incomes; try looking at career advancement from the point of view of a person testing HIV-positive; try looking at housing opportunities from the eyes of a single parent with three children.

5. *Speak up about what you see and what has caused you to weep.* Michelangelo fashioned in the Pietà a Mary who does not clutch her dead son to her bosom. Instead, she extends her arms and offers Jesus to us to behold. She does not privatize her grief but asks us to participate in it. And the participation is always personal, never anonymous.

But the language of tears sometimes asks for expression in the language of words. Criticism of oppressive systems needs to be made public with passionate conviction that the hurt and injustice will no longer be tolerated.

6. *Invite others into the collective sob.* Since our etiquette calls for emotions to be stifled, and since our culture values privacy, it is sometimes appropriate and often appreciated to extend an invitation to others to join a cause. Publicizing the formation of an Amnesty International cell or the need for volunteers at a battered women's shelter is only part of the equation. The other part is networking—putting the right people in touch with the needs that lead to involvement and participation in the hurts of others.

7. *Learn the various ways to weep.* A mother weeps silent tears when she keeps vigil at her sick child's bedside; a father weeps tears of rage when he learns that his son is on drugs; a husband weeps bitter tears when he has been betrayed.

8. *Understand that weeping is not gender-specific.* The poet Robert Bly performs a great service for us all in allowing men in the seminars he conducts to touch base with their grief. That grief is multi-faceted but it includes grief over a boy's (or man's) unreconciled relationship with his father. Sometimes it involves experiencing grief (and tears) in nature. Bly refers to the Latin term *lacrymae rerum* (the tears of things) to convey the capacity of some sights in nature to bring us, automatically, to tears.

9. *Allow someone to weep* with you. Allow another to experience your pain and to weep with you. Dealing with our own suffering and weeping alone never qualifies us to be co-sufferers with anyone else.

10. *Consider the reasons another person offers for weeping.* One person is the business executive Max De Pree. He suggests that these are some things we probably ought to weep about:

+ superficiality

+ a lack of dignity

+ injustice, the flaw that prevents equity

+ great news

+ tenderness

+ a word of thanks

+ separation

✦ arrogance

✦ betrayal of ideas, of principles, of quality

✦ jargon, because it confuses rather than clarifies

✦ the inability of folks to tell the difference between heroes and celebrities

✦ leaders who never say "thank you"

✦ having to work in a job where you are not free to do your best

✦ people who are gifts to the spirit

Did De Pree cause you to think of some reasons to add to his list? Why should *you* weep?

NOTES

The epigraph comes from Max De Pree's book *Leadership Is an Art* (New York: Dell, 1989), 135. See his comments in the last exercise of this chapter.

The stories of Eang Long and Chhean Im appeared in "They Cried Until They Could Not See," *The New York Times Magazine,* June 23, 1991, 24 ff.

The quotations from Dorothee Soelle on suffering can be found in her book titled *Suffering* (Philadelphia: Fortress Press, 1975), 3–4.

Stanley Hauerwas's description of the human connection that can result from suffering comes from his book *Suffering Presence: Theological Reflections on Medicine, the Mentally Handicapped, and the Church* (Notre Dame, IN: University of Notre Dame Press, 1986), 25. He is also the source of the insight about our preference for eliminating the sufferer.

The poem "Common Life" is by Ray Lindquist (Austin, TX: Cold Mountain Press, 1973). It is quoted in Diogenes Allen, *The Traces of God* (Cambridge, MA: Cowley, 1980), 49.

The information on L'Arche Community was taken from Jean Vanier, *Be Not Afraid* (Toronto: Griffin House, 1975).

Walter Brueggemann's insight on giving voice to suffering is found in his book titled *Prophetic Imagination* (Philadelphia: Fortress Press, 1978).

The address of Arn Chorn is found in "I Am Alive Again," excerpts from the address of Arn Chorn to the annual general meeting of Amnesty International, New York, 1988.

St. Basil's comments to the wealthy on the plight of the poor are found in Jim Wallis, *The Call to Conversion: Recovering the Gospel for These Times* (San Francisco: Harper & Row, 1981), 45.

For a further reflection on Mary as the Pietà, see Louis J. Camelli, "Mary, Mother of Sorrows: The Mystery of Comfort and Hope," in *Chicago Studies* 27 (April 1988), 3–15.

The reference to the voice of the victim as God's voice can be found in Matthew Lamb's article "Spirituality and Social Justice," in *Horizons* 10 (1983), 49.

The account from Elie Wiesel is from his book *Night* (New York: Hill & Wang, 1960), 70 ff.

William Sloane Coffin's account can be found in "Alex's Death," in *The Courage to Love* (San Francisco: Harper & Row, 1984), 93–95.

The novel about the young Jesuit in seventeenth-century Japan, *Silence,* is by Shusaku Endo (New York: Taplinger, 1980), 259. I am indebted to Jean Higgins for her fine study of Endo. See her article "The Inner Agon of Endo Shusaku," in *Cross Currents* 32 (Winter 1984–85), 414–426.

Nicholas Berdayaev's philosophy on the paradox of suffering and Iulia de Beausobre's prison account can both be found in her book *Creative Suffering* (Westminster: Dacre Press, 1946), 24, 38—45. Diogenes Allen thoughtfully provided me with this extraordinary story, which I encourage you to read in its entirety.

Robert Bly's comments are recorded in Bill Moyers, *A World of Ideas: II. Public Opinion from Private Citizens,* edited by Andie Tucker (New York: Doubleday, 1990), 275.

Max De Pree's list of reasons to weep comes from his book *Leadership Is an Art,* cited earlier, 138–139.

Chapter 6

LAUGHING

The devil laughs because God's world seems senseless;
the angel laughs with joy because everything
in God's world has meaning.
MILAN KUNDERA, *THE BOOK OF LAUGHTER AND FORGETTING*

A curious custom in the Greek Orthodox tradition gathers believers on Easter Monday for the purpose of trading jokes. Since the most extravagant "joke" of all took place on Easter Sunday—the victory, against all odds, of Jesus over death—the community of the faithful enters into the spirit of the season by sharing stories with unexpected endings, surprise flourishes, and a sense of humor. A similar practice occurs among the Slavs, who recognize in the resurrection of Jesus of Nazareth a joy that it is Jesus who has the last laugh.

Most mainline Christian congregations do not celebrate Easter in quite this way. However, the response of the Greeks and the Slavs seems in some ways more appropriate than our conventional one. Something is wrong with our perception of the alliance between being religious and having a sense of humor.

Yet so many blessings are associated with humor that it is hard to imagine a Christian living without this gift. Perhaps that is the point: Anyone who calls himself or herself Christian and is without a sense of humor may well be taking the name in vain. The exercises in this chapter will do more than make us laugh; they will offer opportunities for us to reinforce our identity as Christians.

OBSTACLES TO HUMOR

Three elements sever the connection between religion and humor and create bona fide obstacles to the critical and desperately needed exercise of humor.

Some people perceive humor as unworthy of the majesty of God. For them, humor is undignified, frivolous, and unbecoming.

Several years ago Umberto Eco's powerful novel *The Name of the Rose* introduced the villainous monk Jorge, who poisoned anyone who came upon the one book in the monastery library that proposed that God laughed. The investigator who uncovered the malice asked Jorge the question on the reader's mind: "But what frightened you in this discussion of laughter? You cannot eliminate laughter by eliminating the book." Jorge defended himself by claiming: "Laughter is weakness, corruption, the foolishness of our flesh [but] the function of laughter is reversed [in this book]: It is elevated to art, the doors of the world of the learned are opened to it, it becomes the object of philosophy, and of perfidious theology."

From Jorge's point of view, the possibility of *anyone* learning *anything* from laughter was intolerable. "I accept the risk of damnation," Jorge boasts. "The Lord will absolve me, because He knows I acted for his glory." Presumably, as a devoted bibliophile, Jorge could not bring himself to eliminate the book itself, which, after all, would have prevented anyone from discovering it. Apparently, eliminating *people* was a less serious offense!

Jorge is an example of someone who feels that the crudity and baseness of humor is inconsistent with the elegance of the Creator God, who needs distance from created humanity. What drove Jorge to desperation, among other things, was the thought that God and humankind could become, if not equals, at least friends through the familiarity humor engenders. A universe where men and women could appreciate the divine folly of God's taking on human nature in the mystery of the Incarnation seemed scandalous to Jorge.

Few would go to the extremes Jorge did, of course, but that same repressive spirit exists among those who reckon laughter and humor to be out of place in theology and worship. Perhaps they confuse humor with comic books and one-liners and miss its depth and insight into human nature. Reinhold Niebuhr reminds us that "humour is, in fact, a prelude to faith, and laughter is the beginning of prayer."

Another obstacle to exercising humor is that laughter is not easy to come by in circles where people speak *for* God and not *to* God. Parents, clergy, and theologians sometimes speak with absolute confidence concerning what God wants, when God will reward, whom God loves, how God will punish, what God thinks, and how God feels.

The Jewish experience of God is frequently (and mercifully) different. A familiarity with God is widely apparent in Judaism along with the acceptance of human emotions before the Deity. Jews have a long history of weeping, moaning, and raging, as well as rejoicing. The liturgical behavior of Christians seems, by comparison, to be considerably more polite and restrained. The conversation of the Jew with God is precisely that: a conversation, with a give-and-take rarely found, if not entirely unheard of, in the Christian way of relating to the Creator.

There is the story of the atheist grandmother claiming Jewish cultural (if not religious) roots who took her beloved five-year-old grandson to the beach. Decked out in his sunsuit and hat, and equipped with his pail and shovel, the little boy played happily near the water, building castles and moats. When the grandmother dozed, the grandson was caught in an undertow, and pulled out to sea; when the grandmother awoke, he was nowhere in sight.

The frantic grandmother called for help, but there was no one else on the beach. Figuring she had nothing to lose, she fell to the ground, raised her arms to heaven, and prayed: "God, if you exist, if you are there, please save my grandson. I promise I'll make it up to you. I'll join the Hadassah; I'll volunteer at the hospital; I'll join the men's club, the women's club, whatever makes you happy." And suddenly a huge wave tossed the grandson on the beach at her feet. The grandmother bent over to hear his heart beating; she noticed color in his cheeks and his eyes opening, but she appeared upset. Bringing herself to full height and with hands on her hips, she wagged her finger at the sky: "He had a hat, you know!"

Humor is possible in this situation only because the grandmother speaks *to* and not *for* God. The repartee is down-to-earth. Fear and domination are missing from the scene. The grandmother knows her place, and God's. It may appear as though she is overstepping her bounds, or that she is disrespectful, but the truth is that it is the person who speaks *for* God who shows disrespect. The grandmother is simply being a grandmother. And in typical Jewish fashion, the God in the story is personalized. God is someone who can be berated and cajoled because God is very much part of the family.

A third obstacle to being a humorous Christian is the pervasive inability to uncover humor in the events recorded in Holy Scripture, especially in the life and death of Jesus of Nazareth. Years of conditioning have rendered the Scriptures predictable and innocuous stories in which serious people speak in a language filled with moralisms and legalisms lacking fun and surprise. The dangerous consequence of reading the Bible this way is that the Creator God and, by extension, Jesus Christ become humorless beings incapable of enjoying a joke. And so do we as their disciples.

Since Jesus was witty, unpredictable, fully alive, and a person who delighted in, celebrated with, and was open to surprise, divorcing humor from religion is potentially destructive of true religion. Even when the separation is done with the best of motives, or in ignorance, the results are disastrous. We rob ourselves of the lightness and freedom necessary to notice and then adore God. It is lightness that allows us to appreciate God; seriousness and heaviness tend to force us to concentrate on ourselves. "Seriousness implies gravity," one wise scholar proposed. "Gravity is the force that pulls all things to the center. It is what keeps us from flying. It is the opposite of levity which is the force that raises things and makes them light. Religion is supposed to free the spirit from gravity, raise it, lighten our loads, and enlighten our minds."

Did Jesus Have a Sense of Humor?

Fortunately for us all, a new lens is being fitted onto biblical interpretation that focuses on a different way to look at salvation history. Many distinguished biblical scholars are finding humor as a key to unlock the meaning of the holy writings. Some are focusing on the parables, while others are unearthing a humorous perspective in the miracle stories. Robert Fowler, for example, attempts to show that Mark's use of miracle stories mocks the quest for power among the disciples as well as among contemporary readers.

The yield of this kind of scholarship is that God and many of the personalities in the Scriptures emerge in full color with refreshing perspectives never before seen by most of us. We see Jesus as one who used irony, played with words, appreciated and exercised wit, and engaged in the cosmic surprise that we call the Incarnation.

Instead of asking "Did Jesus tell jokes?", a far, far better question is "Did Jesus have a sense of humor?" He did. No matter what the Jorges of the world would want us to believe, there is a harmful consequence in not finding humor in the gospel. The tragedy is that we may not only miss the message but that we may receive the wrong message.

Doug Adams, who has spent a great deal of his time uncovering the humor of the Scriptures, illustrates the dilemma and the difference humor makes in his discussion of Matthew 22:15–22, where Jesus is challenged to resolve the issue of paying monies to Caesar. Many conclude that this episode is about the separation of Christian faith from politics. They miss Jesus's sharp humor in eluding the trap laid by the Pharisees and his clever unmasking of their hypocrisy.

Reading the passage afresh, we notice that when Jesus asks the Pharisees to produce a coin, they do so, even though a strictly pious Jew would never carry a coin bearing Caesar's image with an inscription proclaiming Caesar to be king and God. These presumed righteous citizens carrying around coins break two commandments! The behavior of the Pharisees is incriminating, embarrassing, and amusing. Robert Funk also points out that there is no indication that Jesus returned the coin to the Pharisee. According to Funk, as Jesus proclaims the punchline—"And [give] to God the things that are God's" (Matt. 22:21)—he pockets the coin and has the last laugh.

MAINTAINING OUR BALANCE

We need to be very careful defining humor because humor tends to die in the process of dissection. Elusive as it is, humor is generally understood to involve two elements: a gentle acceptance of the incongruities of life and the ability not to take ourselves too seriously. The root of the English word *humor* is the Latin *umor*, meaning "liquid, fluid." Humor is something that flows within us and courses through us with the ability to refresh perspective, heal attitudes, and balance our equilibrium. The *American Heritage Dictionary* calls it "a capacity to appreciate or understand."

Through humor we understand, appreciate, and even embrace those many puzzling, curious, and mismatched events and occurrences that permeate our daily existence. The comedian Woody Allen has a particular genius for pointing out these incongruities. In *The Nightclub Years*, he tells us that his parents' values are "God and carpeting"; in *Take the Money and Run*, his mother-in-law has a conversation with God about "salvation and interior decorating."

The sublime and the ridiculous, or the expected and the surprising, are paired—that is incongruity. Our contemplation of these juxtapositions is integral to humor.

Not all incongruities, however, are funny or entertaining. Most of us can think of tragic "incongruities" that have happened to friends or family, like when twin sons of a musically gifted mother and father are born deaf. When we are face-to-face with incongruities such as these, obviously laughter or joke telling is not appropriate. "To laugh at life in the ultimate sense is to scorn it," Reinhold Niebuhr wrote. But what *is* a fitting response is to step back and gain balance, perspective, and a sense of proportion. The incongruities of life do not need to defeat us. An ultimate victory over powers that seem insurmountable *is* possible.

The Christian faith is so filled with incongruities (the weak inherit the earth, the foolish teach wisdom, the lame are restored to wholeness, death leads to life, a virgin gives birth) that it is hard to imagine how one could be religious and *not* have a sense of humor.

DIVINE INCONGRUITY: THE IMPOSSIBLE BECOMES POSSIBLE

The most extraordinary incongruity of all, of course, is the Incarnation: God takes on flesh and human nature. The impossible becomes possible: a king is born in a stable, a child upsets the entrenched political establishment, the Savior is servant of all. Saint Paul wrote about this "divine incongruity": "Though he was in the form of God, [Jesus] did not regard equality with God as something to be exploited, but emptied himself, taking the form of a slave" (Phil. 2:5b–7a).

The history of the early Church chronicles a lengthy list of heresies that denied, compromised, or confused the teaching concerning the God-man Jesus Christ. Some believers gracefully accepted and embraced the event in which God became one of us in all things but sin, but many did not.

A sense of humor may well be a sign of God's presence in the life of a believer, but it is a gift always in jeopardy of being lost. Perhaps that is why many have prayed for it, prizing it above all other gifts. Danish philosopher Søren Kierkegaard (of all people!) claimed he could not live without humor. On one occasion, he wrote of a dream he had when he was young:

> Something marvelous has happened to me. I was caught up into the seventh heaven. There sat all the gods in assembly. As a special grace, there was accorded to me the privilege of making a wish. "Wilt thou," said Mercury, "wilt thou have youth, or beauty, or power, or long life, or the most beautiful maiden, or any other glorious thing among the many we have here—in the treasure chest? Then choose but one thing." For an instant, I was irresolute, then I addressed the gods as follows: "Highly esteemed contemporaries, I choose one

thing, that I may always have the laugh on my side."
There was not a god that answered a word, but they all
burst out laughing. Thereupon, I concluded that my
wish was granted, and I found that gods knew how to
express themselves with good taste.

The gift of being able to accept incongruity is still a gift worth
seeking—for ourselves, for our families and friends, and for leaders of
nations, too. The grace to behold and embrace incongruities is the
beginning of acquiring the endangered sense of humor.

HUMOR AS AN AFFIRMATION OF FREEDOM

A sense of humor is also a precondition of holiness. Holiness is
about the discovery of the self and of God. For those discoveries to
happen, we must get out of the way, loosen our grip, lessen our need
to control, and let God be God. A sense of humor helps the sanctifica-
tion process because it encourages us not to take ourselves too seriously. Taking ourselves too seriously deals a lethal blow to holiness.

A life of prayer involves the serious and painful transformation
into what (or, more precisely, who) we love. The target of holiness is
precisely that false self that is comfortable on the run, evading the
truth, settling for fraudulent and impoverished existence.

When we face the truth about ourselves there is no room for arrogance or self-absorption. More than one person has pointed out how
close *humility* and *humor* are. A sense of humor, like a true sense of
humility, involves ruthless honesty about who we are without disguise
or pretense. The temptation is to become weighted with gravity, to
deal with prayer and worship with excessive formality, and to take ourselves too seriously. The opposite route is the direct one. The grace
needed is to face ourselves with an appropriate degree of lightness so
that we can listen obediently to the plan God has for each of us.

We are singularly gifted in avoiding self-discovery, even though we
pay lip service to "letting it all hang out" and "telling it like it is." Impressed with our self-importance and the seriousness of the adventure

of self-discovery, we are sitting ducks for missing the meaning of what is going on. Shock therapy is frequently called for.

The parables of the New Testament have functioned as shock treatments for centuries, providing insight and revelation about ourselves as unmasked before God. But Thomas Merton (among many others) found in Zen a way of fostering disclosure we too often bypass in the Gospels. Sometimes a different tradition catches us off guard and lets us see what we are skilled at circumventing in the world, a world we are able to manipulate. Thus, Merton tells this story:

A Zen master said to his disciples: "Go get my rhinoceros-horn fan."

Disciple: "Sorry, Master, it is broken."

Master: "Okay, then get me the rhinoceros."

On the journey of becoming what we were meant to be, we need to let go of preconceived notions, plans, schemes, and patterns. We need to suspend logic. A new order of meaning takes over and we need to be humble enough and have sense of humor enough to accept that.

From the outside looking in, this exchange is a transparent contest of wills. From the outside looking in, humor abounds. The disciple must flow with the event and not strain against its apparent absurdity. There are secrets to be learned in such moments. The impending enlightenment has to do with the power of God and our capacity for self-deception, which cannot be learned on our own terms but rather only through the silence, detachment, and purity of heart that invite God to be present.

But if the wisdom of the Zen approach is apparent to the outsider, it can be painful, frustrating, and stressful to the one on the inside. All of the conventions and rules have been changed. There is no question that a transcendent power, not we, is in charge. Control must be abandoned. Surrender is necessary.

In the flush of letting go, a death occurs. It is the death of the ego and a death of the familiar, ego-centered order we superimpose on reality. And this is precisely where a sense of humor enters—or ought to enter—the picture. Without it, we may fearfully retreat into our self-pitying, pompous, or safe selves ready to share the harrowing experience of what almost happened with anyone who will listen. Without a sense of humor, an imprisonment occurs that shackles the human spirit and turns it in on itself in an aggrandized version of its self-importance.

But humor, Peter Berger reminds us, is an affirmation of freedom and an indication that no system or event is able to contain the human spirit. A sense of humor is the saving grace that allows life to emerge from ashes. It is what Berger calls a "signal of transcendence." The moment of enlightenment on the part of the Zen disciple is not only a death, it is also a birth. The "Aha!" of recognition signals a rebirth of ourselves as stronger than we imagined, and more joyful. Here is Merton again on the subject:

> [The true self] is like a very shy wild animal that never appears at all whenever an alien presence is at hand, and comes out only when all is peaceful, . . . when he is untroubled and alone. He cannot be lured by anyone or anything, because he responds to no lure except that of the divine freedom.

The freedom Merton talks about is precisely the heart of humor. To be free is to laugh at the false self, the certain self, the vain self. To be free is to stake everything on God, to risk one's life, to bank on God's promises, because humor restores God to center stage.

Threatened and frightened people will protect all kinds of things: possessions, reputations, status, achievements. But redeemed women and men will count everything as "folly" except service of the Lord. If that doesn't require a sense of humor, nothing I know does.

"A Cheerful Heart Is a Good Medicine"

Humor produces good health. Proverbs 17:22 suggests that "a cheerful heart is a good medicine," and several physicians who have done research in this area agree. Physician Raymond A. Moody writes provocatively of the healing effects of humor. In some cases of mental illness, especially depression, he believes humor has been a vital part of the healing process. Dr. Moody holds firmly to the conviction that humor is widely recognized as an important, healthy, and desirable response. One particularly touching example cited by Dr. Moody is the use of humor by patients who have received disfiguring facial injuries. Humor not only helps these patients to develop an outlook that makes their misfortune seem more bearable, but it also helps them to solve problems in interpersonal communication. Humor defuses tension in such situations and puts everyone at ease.

Another American physician, William F. Fry, has studied the effect humor has in producing the alertness hormones catecholamines. These hormones cause the release of endorphins in the brain. Endorphins foster a sense of relaxation and well-being and dull the perception of pain. Catecholamines also enhance blood flow, which can speed healing, reduce inflammation, and stimulate alertness.

For cardiovascular and respiratory functions, the effect of laughter is especially significant. When we laugh, our rhythmic breathing becomes spasmodic. Heart rate, blood pressure, and muscular tension increase. When laughter subsides, however, these functions often drop temporarily below normal, resulting in feelings of relaxation that may last as long as forty-five minutes after the last laugh. Preliminary research in this area suggests that laughter may be a powerful weapon in counteracting heart disease and high blood pressure.

Laughter is also associated with the will to live. While scientific research in this area is still in its early stages, there seems to be a growing sense of appreciation for Mark Twain's observation of the old man who "laughed loud and joyously, shook up the details of his anatomy from head to foot, and ended by saying that such a laugh was money in a man's pocket, because it cut down the doctor's bills like everything."

In addition to health, there are other prominent benefits of humor worth mentioning. Shakespeare's Hamlet best calls them to our attention. Hamlet mourns:

> I have of late . . . lost all mirth . . . it goes so heavily
> with my disposition that this goodly frame, the earth,
> seems to me a sterile promontory. . . . Man delights
> me not—no, nor woman neither.

There is much to learn from Hamlet. For one thing, he points to a crucial benefit of humor, namely, *balance*. This is a benefit that eludes the Prince of Denmark. There is plenty of sadness, gloom, and misery in his life, but there is little, if any, joy, spontaneity, or fun to offset the heaviness. Balance is a necessary support for healthy living. It means that there is some equality on both the debit and credit sides of the ledger. A balanced person is usually tolerant, with a wide range of tastes, and is not swayed to either extreme.

A second benefit of humor is *perspective*. It is possible to keep it, gain it, or lose it. Keeping or gaining perspective is positive. It means that we are reading reality accurately. Someone who has lost perspective is no longer able to report the world with fairness and objectivity because his or her judgment is impaired.

The gracious gift of humor jiggles perspective and coaches us not to be too anxious. Tension not only keeps us from seeing the humor in a situation; it also obscures God's presence in our lives. It could be that Woody Allen is on to something when he suggests that the secret of the universe is "Not to yodel."

Third, by upsetting conventional ways of doing things, humor gives us *opportunities for creativity*. Like prayer, humor deals with surprises that upset the way things are or ought to be. The first letter to the people of Corinth says that "God chose what is foolish in the world to shame the wise: God chose what is weak in the world to shame the strong" (1 Cor. 1:27–28). That kind of paradoxical choice fits hand-in-glove with the creativity possible through humor. We reach for new approaches and find that they are within our grasp. In humor the freedom and spontaneity of the person are exalted.

EXERCISING LAUGHTER

The divine quality of humor is poking its fragile head through centuries of humorless Christianity. In the interest of spontaneity and surprise, and in order to strengthen and revitalize one's sense of humor, here are some recommendations:

1. *Stretch your imagination to look for humor.* It is possible in almost every situation. And realize that humor is not the same as laughter or telling jokes. The world is filled with people who tell jokes—mostly at the expense of others—but who have no sense of humor.

2. *Take inventory of a situation causing pain.* If you don't know where to begin, seek the advice of someone who is joyful and gifted with a sense of humor. Humor lightens the heaviness associated with hurt. Humor doesn't deny the hurt; it is the vehicle through which anger and defiance and pain are handled. Peter Berger writes: "By laughing at the imprisonment of the human spirit, humor implies that the imprisonment is not final but will be overcome."

3. *Spend time with people who have a sense of humor;* their perspective will be contagious. Spend time with people who laugh at themselves. Anyone can laugh at another's stupidity; it takes a special gift of self-awareness and self-consciousness to recognize folly in ourselves.

4. *Practice laughing.* Psalm 2 says that God laughs. What God does must be good for us, too, so look for occasions to laugh and then *do* it. Laughter loosens up the diaphragm, which is in contact with all the other vital organs of the body. When we laugh, all these organs are massaged. It could be that our spirits get massaged, too. It is important to know the difference between phony laughter and the real kind. The Czech novelist Milan Kundera notes that "the devil laughs because God's world seems senseless; the angel laughs with joy because everything in God's world has meaning."

5. *Practice verbal disarmament.* The ancient art of aikido, one form of the Eastern martial arts, invites blending with your opponent rather than defeating him or her. Aikido prohibits aggression and asks for a graceful response to potential insult or injury. So does aikido's modern equivalent, "tongue fu." For example, when the humorist Robert Benchley asked a uniformed gentleman outside a restaurant to hail a cab for him, the man was indignant. "Do you realize you are speaking to a rear admiral in the United States Navy?" Mr. Benchley's swift reply: "OK, then, get me a battleship."

6. *Take a five-to-ten-minute laugh break every day.* Why not? We already take refreshment breaks, and there is general consensus that humor is refreshing. Read one of the books connected with the humor of Pope John XXIII. It was he who once wryly reminisced that there are three surefire ways to lose money—carousing, gambling, and farming—and that his own father had chosen the most boring route.

7. *Realize that an alliance exists between laughter and communication with God.* The American novelist Frederick Buechner traces his interest in religion to a sermon by George Buttrick. In that homily, Buttrick proclaimed that Christ is crowned in the hearts of believers "among confession and tears and great laughter." It was the phrase "great laughter," Buechner says, that caught his attention and held it.

8. The last suggestion may be the most important of all: *Look for humor in the Scriptures.* The Old and New Testaments brim with humor that we often overlook because of patterns of conditioning that are hard to break. Be prepared to be surprised. Relax. Read the Bible open to the possibility that something new is happening—that God lives in laughter, lightness, freedom, spontaneity, and some unfamiliar places.

And refuse to believe anyone who tells you otherwise.

NOTES

The epigraph is from Milan Kundera, *The Book of Laughter and Forgetting* (New York: Penguin, 1981), 232.

For the story about the custom among the Greek Orthodox community, see Conrad Hyers, "Easter Hilarity," in *And God Created Laughter: The Bible as Divine Comedy* (Atlanta: John Knox Press, 1987), 24–28.

See Umberto Eco's book *The Name of the Rose* (New York: Harcourt Brace Jovanovich, 1983), 474 and 471, for direct quotations.

C. S. Lewis also saw a connection between laughter and the devil, although he approached the subject in a way different from Eco. See his book *The Screwtape Letters* (New York: Macmillan paperback edition, 1974), 50.

Reinhold Niebuhr is quoted from his essay "Humour and Faith," in *Discerning the Signs of the Times* (New York: Scribner's, 1946), 111. See also 126.

The source for the story about the grandmother and her grandson is "Meditations on a Joyful Year, Speed Vogel Talks with Moshe Waldoks," in *Parabola* 12 (Winter 1987), 63.

For the quotation about gravity, see Stanley M. Handelman, "From the Sublime to the Ridiculous: The Religion of Humor," in *Handbook of Humor Research*, edited by Paul E. McGhee and Jeffrey H. Goldstein (New York: Springer-Verlag, 1983), 27.

On the subject of humor and the Scriptures, some particularly helpful sources are the works of John Dominic Crossan, especially: *In Parables: The Challenge of the Historical Jesus* (San Francisco: Harper & Row, 1973); *Raid on the Articulate: Comic Eschatology in Jesus and Borges* (San Francisco: Harper & Row, 1976); *The Dark Interval: Towards a Theology of Story* (Allen, TX: Argus/DLM Communications, 1975). See also Dan O. Via, *Kerygma and Comedy in the New Testament* (Philadelphia: Fortress Press, 1975). Of particular pastoral interest is Michael Moynahan's *Once Upon a Parable: Story Dramatizations of Jesus' Parables of the Kingdom of God* (Mahwah, NJ: Paulist Press, 1984) and the creative application of scholarship by Doug Adams in "Bringing Biblical Humor to Life in Liturgy," *Modern Liturgy* 6 (8) (May 1984), 4–5, 27–29.

See Robert Fowler, *Loaves and Fishes: The Function of the Feeding Stories in the Gospel of Mark* (New York: Scholars Press, 1981).

Robert Funk's insight about Caesar's coin is quoted in the Adams article, cited earlier, 5.

I found helpful an article by Gary Commins, "Woody Allen's Theological Imagination," *Theology Today* 44 (July 1987), 235–249, especially 235 and 243.

The Kierkegaard quotation is cited in E. Van Hoboken, *Sengai* (Greenwich, CT: New York Graphic Society, 1971), 6.

On the subject of control, Sigmund Freud and the philosopher Henri Bergson are in agreement. Both hold humor to be the breakdown of control. For Freud, the joke or the humorous situation provides the opportunity for relaxation of the conscious control in favor of the subconscious. Bergson and Freud saw humor as an attack on routine and the predictable. See Henri Bergson, "Laughter," in *Comedy,* edited by W. Sypher (Baltimore, MD: Johns Hopkins University Press, 1956), 61–190, and Sigmund Freud, *Jokes and Their Relation to the Unconscious,* translated by J. Strachey (New York: Norton, 1983), 144–158.

Thomas Merton's story of the rhinoceros can be found in *Zen and the Birds of Appetite* (New York: New Directions, 1968), 13–14.

Peter Berger's famous observation about signals of transcendence is located in *A Rumor of Angels* (New York: Doubleday, 1969), 88. See also his *The Precarious Vision* (Westport, CT: Greenwood Press, 1961; reissued 1981), 209 ff.

"The Inner Experience: Notes on Contemplation" (an unpublished manuscript), quoted in James Finley, *Merton's Palace of Nowhere* (Notre Dame, IN: Ave Maria Press, 1978), is the source of the quotation about the true self.

In his book *Laugh after Laugh: The Healing Power of Humor* (Jacksonville, FL: Headwaters Press, 1987), Raymond A. Moody, Jr., M.D., writes of humor and the curative process. See especially 25–26.

The reporting about Dr. Fry and the beneficial effects of laughter on cardiovascular and respiratory patients comes from the "Personal Health" column by Jane E. Brody in *The New York Times* (National Edition), April 7, 1988, 18. Ms. Brody is also the source of the Robert Benchley story later in my text.

Mark Twain, *The Adventures of Tom Sawyer* (New York: Modern Library edition, 1940), 208, is the source of the quotation about the man who "shook up the details of his anatomy."

Hamlet's lament is from act 2, scene 2, of *Hamlet.*

See Woody Allen, "Fabulous Tales and Mythical Beasts," in *Without Feathers* (New York: Random House, 1975), 181, for the yodeling quotation.

Peter Berger, *A Rumor of Angels* (New York: Doubleday, 1969), 88, is the source for his comment.

The comment made by Kundera is in *The Book of Laughter and Forgetting,* cited in the epigraph, 232. Kundera continues: "Two lovers race through the meadow, holding hands, laughing. Their laughter . . . is the *serious* laughter of angels expressing their job of being" (233; his italics). Note also the titles of two other books by Kundera: *The Joke* and *Laughable Loves.*

A Pope Laughs: Stories of John XXIII, collected by Kurt Klinger (New York: Holt, Rinehart & Winston, 1964), 110, is the source of Pope John XXIII's remark.

For the George Buttrick reference, see Frederick Buechner, *The Sacred Journey* (New York: Walker & Co., 1984), 109.

Chapter 7

FORGIVING

Forgiveness is the answer to the child's dream of a
miracle by which what is broken is made whole again.
DAG HAMMARSKJÖLD, *MARKINGS*

The woman seated across from me in the Denver hotel lobby spoke softly, as if raising her voice above a whisper would diminish the impact of her revelation. She asked to see me after she heard me lecture on the subject of forgiveness because she was sure she could identify an offense so despicable that it could be considered unforgivable. "No matter what the Bible says," she interjected several times, "there are some things that do not deserve forgiveness."

About a year before our meeting, the woman's thirty-five-year-old husband had admitted to sexually abusing their five-year-old daughter. The disclosure had torn the woman apart and had led her to the brink of a nervous breakdown.

In hindsight, the clues had been there all along: her husband's willingness to stay at home with their daughter when the child was not feeling well; his eagerness to have his wife take the night shift at the restaurant she managed; her daughter's inexplicable withdrawal and listlessness. But the woman had made no connections.

Even when a physician had presented the facts and suggested foul play, "probably from someone close," she had defended her husband. "I trusted my husband," she said. "I never suspected anything."

A year of family therapy had brought them no closer to healing the wounds that divided them. The possibility of a reconciliation seemed unlikely, and forgiveness, even more remote. The woman before me was especially adamant about forgiveness. To forgive her husband (or to encourage her daughter to forgive her father) would, she felt, condone the deed; it would say that what he did was not that awful; and worst of all, it might send a message that the offense could be repeated.

Every one of her friends agreed, she assured me, and all of her family did, too.

She wondered what I thought.

And I wonder the same about you.

Headlines in our newspapers tell us that tragic occurrences like this one are not uncommon. Sometimes we know, firsthand, of humanity's inhumanity. And backed up against perversity, we know that the Jewish-Christian heritage calls us to forgive.

Like the woman in the hotel lobby, all of us at one time or another have had a hard time reconciling the simple logic that inclines us to withhold forgiveness with the religious imperative that calls us to forgive. The exercises in this chapter will open us to offer forgiveness and ready us to receive it. Forgiveness is difficult. Ignoring that it involves struggles makes forgiveness a fanciful, silly, and weak activity. Forgiveness then becomes the last resort among spineless and powerless individuals who do not know how to move out of the role of victim. Forgiveness, then, is not to be taken as a serious option.

FORGIVENESS IS UNREASONABLE

Forgiveness *is* unreasonable behavior. We need to concede that at the outset. In its simplest expression, it says that I choose not to hold what you did against you, but rather that I wipe the slate clean and do not allow your offense to stand in the way of our relationship. It says that failures—even big ones—are redeemable, and that what is broken can be mended or made whole again. That kind of attitude defies logic and common sense.

Far more reasonable, of course, is a policy not to forgive grave offenses. Such a judgment would be respected and justified under most circumstances. After all, none of us are morally obliged to forgive others. It is our prerogative to forgive or not to forgive: we choose.

It is only in the context of the Judeo-Christian tradition that we see forgiveness as an obligation. Jews and Christians hinge the obligation on a theology that reveals a God who is "slow to anger, and abounding in steadfast love, and relents from punishing" (Joel 2:13). With compassion and mercy, this God welcomes the sinner back, makes sins that were scarlet as white as snow, forgives without any strings attached, forgives *anything*. The power of God's forgiveness is especially evident in the ability to distance the offender from the offense—"as far as the east is from the west, so far [God] removes our transgressions from us" (Ps. 102)—a euphemism that suggests that the distance is marked by infinity.

FORGIVENESS RESTORES SELF-RESPECT

In the New Testament, Jesus reinforced what the prophets and the psalmist said in the Old: he taught in words and by example that forgiveness was going to be the benchmark of his disciples. Often enough, Jesus himself initiated the act of forgiveness before anyone thought of asking. He extended forgiveness to a paralyzed man who came for a cure of his illness; perhaps reaffirming the connection between physical and spiritual healing, perhaps owning that the spiritual paralysis was symptomatic of the physical disability (Mark 2:1-12). He forgave an uninvited guest at dinner at Simon's house and held up her loving behavior as exemplary. Jesus went a long way in restoring the self-respect and self-worth of those he forgave. Jesus may have abhorred the sin, but he loved the sinner. When he forgave the woman at Simon's house, Jesus was able to separate her from her past, her reputation, and her sin by "owning" the person and "disowning" the sin—a pattern of reconciliation that has been part of the Church community since then (see Luke 7:36-50).

Jesus forgave because he was a free man; so radically and totally free, in fact, that he was not concerned with losing face, or with being hurt again. He did not need to insist on a probation policy toward offenders. When Jesus forgave, it was an unconditional display of love and acceptance offered with no strings attached. Jesus made it clear that once forgiven, the negative deed would not stand in the way of the relationship. We don't earn forgiveness, and we don't deserve it. It is a totally free offer whereby God loves us, accepts us, and heals us.

And it is God's activity as forgiver that we are called to imitate. It is as simple, and as difficult, as that.

Some people give concrete witness to the struggle involved in imitating God's example. Terry Anderson, an American who was held hostage in Iran for six and a half years, is one of those. Composed and serene at a lengthy press conference in Wiesbaden, Germany, after his release on December 4, 1991, Anderson assessed his confinement and acknowledged that the behavior of those who held and tortured him was wrong, very wrong. Blindfolded, chained to furniture, beaten, wrapped like a corpse in adhesive tape for his transfers from one hiding place to the next, Anderson had every cause to hate in return. It is unlikely that anyone in the room full of reporters that day would have begrudged him a wish to retaliate, harm, or punish his oppressors. But Anderson spoke quietly of forgiveness and forgoing vengeance. "I don't hate anybody," he said. "I'm a Christian and it's required of me to forgive, no matter how hard it might be."

When Terry Anderson identifies us as people called to imitate God's forgiving behavior, he does not dismiss the difficulties but deals with them from a particular vantage point. He helps us to find in that vantage point a logic that surpasses the substantial logic and appeal of the secular world, which holds forgiveness as preposterous, unnecessary, and in some cases, imperative to withhold.

The teachings of Jesus and the testimony of Terry Anderson make a case for the healthy appropriation of an exercise called forgiving.

FORGIVING CANCELS A DEBT

The world of banking and finance gives us a clue about the nature of forgiveness. In those circles, to forgive a loan, for example, means to expunge it from the books, to cancel the debt attached, to act as though it never existed. Forgiving the debt means looking at the ledger and declaring that the balance owed is zero.

The same principle holds true in the act of forgiveness. The offender owes something to the victim or to society—an apology, certainly, or another form of contrition indicating a change of heart. The offender also "owes" some gesture at balancing the scales knocked out of whack by the misdeed. Once part of the "problem," the offender needs to be part of the "solution." He may need to make restitution for his behavior through community service or by accepting a suspension of some privilege (the revocation of a driver's license, participation in therapy aimed at coming to terms with the offense, or even a jail term).

Practically speaking, of course, the offender cannot "pay back" what is really owed, nor can he truly undo the past. In some cases, like the injustices and inequities endured by African and Native Americans or the extermination of six million Jews during the Third Reich, undoing the past is impossible. No amount of punishment will bring those killed in the Holocaust back to life, no penalty will restore African-American victims of racist groups, and nothing can undo the physical harm done to a sexually molested child. It is precisely that desperation and frustration that is part of the suffering of the victims and their families.

True forgiveness always means that a debt has been canceled and that the slate has been wiped clean. When the community required Hester Prynne to wear a scarlet letter *A* to acknowledge her adultery, it was clear that her neighbors perceived that a debt was still pending and that they were deficient as forgivers. Nathaniel Hawthorne's *Scarlet Letter* is a powerful story that exposes mean-spirited people who continue to embarrass and harass the offender. Saint Paul warned against this kind of excessive punishment lest the offender "be overwhelmed by excessive sorrow" (2 Cor. 2:7). To her credit, Hester Prynne rose above them all, accepting the unfair double standard that accused her and ignored her partner. She maintained her peace and dignity.

To refuse to release the offender from the offense contradicts what forgiveness is. The Greek verb *aphienai*, which we translate as "to forgive," is more accurately translated as "to dismiss" or "to release."

On the other side of things, the one who "forgoes" or forgives the debt understands that ultimate justice is not in her hands. That privilege belongs to God. So she loosens her grip in demanding vengeance while at the same time recognizes the common sense (and moral sense) of the need for help for the offender. And she does not get in the way of that. Her forgiving attitude, however, will gradually allow her to surrender resentment and the need to punish. Her forgiving attitude will help her to choose a course of action not geared to humiliate someone or eke out revenge. Her sincere forgiving attitude allows her to be confrontative, direct, and forgiving at the same time. Firmness, she discovers, is not incompatible with forgiveness, and it is even part of the routine of life in the New Testament.

A Strategy from Matthew

A blueprint for this kind of confrontative behavior is, in fact, detailed in the Gospel of Matthew, Chapter 18. The relevant verses are these:

> If another member of the church sins against you, go and point out the fault when the two of you are alone. If the member listens to you, you have regained that one. But if you are not listened to, take one or two others along with you, so that every word may be confirmed by the evidence of two or three witnesses. If the member refuses to listen to them, tell it to the church; and if the offender refuses to listen even to the church, let such a one be to you as a Gentile and a tax collector. (v. 15–17)

Note how the passage from Matthew offers a layered plan of action. First, a private meeting between the victim and the offender is necessary. There the victim makes known that he or she wants the injurious or destructive behavior to cease. It is the victim who takes the first step in the reconciling effort. Presumably, there is hope for repentance and restoration once the air is cleared, the cards are on the table, and the complaint is made known. It is possible, according to Matthew, that this will be enough to settle the dispute . . . and you will have succeeded in your mission of winning back the offender (v. 15).

Then again, it may not be enough. In that case, the Gospel offers a second course of action. If the offender does not listen, return with one or two witnesses (v. 16). The witnesses are present to strengthen the disapproval of the deed. Their goal is to restore the offender with the community. It is important to note that no part of Matthew's strategy can be used as a technique for one-upmanship or any form of grandstanding. It must not be a way to humiliate the offender, however tempting that option might be, because those motives would disturb the essential goal of reconciliation and peacemaking.

If the first two methods fail, it may be necessary to tell the story to the community so that its total moral weight might be brought to bear on the offender to encourage a mending of his or her ways (v. 17).

It is not at all a sure thing to assume that positive results will follow from this encounter either. Out of weakness, anger, spite, ignorance, fear, or hatred, the offender may choose to continue his or her sinful habit. Then what? The gospel then moves on to step number four and what may at first glance seem to be a harsh move. Matthew advises expulsion from the community.

How this ostracism works is not amplified in Matthew, but the spirit of the expulsion is to render the offender capable of contrition and repentance with an eye toward reconciliation—in the future, if not immediately. This is a refreshing change from the "turn the other cheek" caricature that has distorted the process of forgiveness and has made it appear to be an event without backbone, muscle, or strength. The tone in Matthew's Gospel, on the other hand, is firm and bracing but compassionate as well.

AN EYE FOR AN EYE DOESN'T WORK

Matthew's insight links forgiving behavior with strength and shatters the perception that forgiveness is passive. It nullifies the concept that hate and revenge are the better routes.

Armed with Matthew's wisdom, an insight emerges for the victim that opposes the "eye for an eye" approach. The one called to forgive sees that revenge simply does not work. True, it may temporarily ease the pain, but even a $1-million damage suit will not resurrect a dead daughter to her loving parents. Divorcing an unfaithful husband will not heal the pain of betrayal. Eliminating someone from a will does not ease the hurt that prompted the punitive action in the first place. The exhilaration one may feel as a result of retaliation is short-lived. Revenge may be sweet, but it is ultimately unsatisfying.

Two other insights as well come to light for the forgiver. Yielding the resentment and revenge is of value to the forgiver. We have a tendency to see this the other way around. We are inclined to see forgiveness as a soft response to injury, benefiting principally, if not solely, the offender—letting him off the hook, or not teaching her a lesson.

The benefit of surrendering grudges, resentments, and even hatred accrues mostly to the forgiver. The forgiver is no longer bound in a vicious cycle of always being on the alert to get even. And when she lets go, she often finds that she sleeps better, eats better, relates better, and loves better. Plotting revenge is exhausting; yielding revenge is energizing. Forgiveness redirects energy from revenge and channels it into more constructive enterprises.

VICTIM AND OFFENDER HAVE A COMMON BOND

The second insight that gradually comes to light for the forgiver concerns the residual penalty connected with the hurtful deed. Initially, the victim may feel that the offender can compensate for the damage done, but she gradually comes to see that this will never be. The particular wisdom that emerges for the Christian believer at times like this is that it is Jesus Christ who fully atones the penalty and pays the ransom for all sins, small and large. The atonement and ransom take place in the context of the death of Jesus, who, as an innocent victim, shed his blood for the remission of all sins. We are all sinners, though perhaps some of us more so than others, and we all share in the forgiveness of our sins through the suffering and death of the Christ.

The forgiver comes to recognize that she is more like the offender than she previously thought. Like the offender, she, too, is in need of

God's forgiveness. And in receiving the forgiveness she needs from God, she assumes a responsibility to pass that on to someone in need of forgiveness from her—even if she believes those sins were more heinous than her own.

The obligation for the Christian to forgive is an invitation to imitate Jesus, who forgave unconditionally even when there was no gesture of repentance from the aggressor. "Father, forgive them; for they do not know what they are doing" (Luke 23:34). It is also an invitation to the victim to participate in the redemptive and restorative love of God, which will, of course, be extended to the repentant sinner whether we assent to it or not.

When the offender expresses sorrow and offers restitution, it is a little easier to imagine forgiveness and reconciliation taking place. But the teaching of Jesus says that forgiveness ought to apply even if the offender does not express regret.

Martin Luther King, Jr., comes to mind. King urged African Americans to forgive their uncontrite persecutors, because he understood that the victim must make the first move. To do otherwise is to get caught in the formidable power of hatred. "Hate is a cancer," King wrote, "and it is capable of destroying the person who hates."

When the victim forgives, that is only one side of the equation. The other side is that the offender needs to receive forgiveness for the reconciliation to be complete. Receiving forgiveness takes place through a turning around, a conversion—to use the technical theological term. When God forgives, as God always does, it is necessary to accept that forgiveness through an act of repentance. And when one person forgives another, the forgiveness needs to be accepted as well for the act to come full circle.

The prior truth is that we are urged to forgive, even when there is no contrition, and we are encouraged to forgive even if we are not certain that our forgiveness will be accepted. It is important to dismantle barriers and to make it crystal clear that an outstretched hand is offered in reconciliation. To do otherwise is to be co-opted in a chain of unforgiveness that recycles resentment and pain and from which we need to be unhooked.

FORGIVENESS IS POWER

Forgiveness is an act marked by sufficient power to release people from the chain of nonforgiveness that holds them captive. Forgiveness says there is a way out of the spiral of violence, and it allows relationships to start anew—fresh and unfettered by the past.

Martin Luther King, Jr., used the teachings of Jesus to show how forgiveness is a power. For him, the power lay in its capacity to change an enemy into a friend.

The one who is hurt consciously chooses to separate the offender from the offense and to hate the deed and not the doer. This is tricky business, but what it amounts to is seeing the person who inflicted the pain as a person of unhealed hurts of her own, who through ignorance or fear is not free to love. Certainly, this attitude is not the instinctive approach to injury. Rather, it operates on the principle that "we do not get rid of an enemy by meeting hate with hate; we get rid of an enemy by getting rid of enmity."

For this to happen, it is imperative for the victim to see the enemy as not totally evil. It is crucial that we operate on the principle that "there is some good in the worst of us and some evil in the best of us" and that "we love our enemies by realizing that they are not totally bad and that they are not beyond the reach of God's redemptive love." Certainly this effort must be tough going when atrocious behavior would suggest that an unforgivable crime had been committed. But it is then that the testimony of Martin Luther King, Jr., is especially persuasive. If Dr. King, who unquestionably had his share of enemies, was convinced of the possibility of the power of forgiveness to change enmity into friendship, its potential is difficult to doubt.

LES MISÉRABLES

The power of forgiveness to effect a new identity for the one forgiven is unforgettably unveiled in Victor Hugo's classic *Les Misérables*. In both the novel and the stunning current theatrical adaptation, the central conflict throbs between two men who represent opposing forces in the universe—the power of compassion and generosity in the life of Jean Valjean and the power of vengeance and retribution in the life of Jean Javert.

Released from prison after serving a nineteen-year sentence for stealing a loaf of bread, Jean Valjean is treated as an outcast. When the kind bishop of Digne befriends him, Valjean, who has interiorized an identity as a thief, behaves accordingly and steals from his benefactor. The bishop, however, refuses to acknowledge the crime to the police. Instead, he not only allows Valjean to keep the stolen goods but also adds a costly silver candelabra to the pack. All items, sold for cash, would presumably provide Valjean with the wherewithal to get settled in a new life.

The bishop tells Valjean that he has claimed his soul for God: "Jean Valjean, my brother, you no longer belong to evil but to good. It is your soul I am buying for you . . . and I give it to God." The compassion of this exceptional person is not lost on Valjean. It is, in fact, transformative.

On the other side of things, Jean Javert is Valjean's nemesis. Of him, Victor Hugo writes that among some peasants there exists the belief that in every litter of wolves there is one born and killed by the mother lest on growing up it should devour the other little ones. "Give a human face to this son of a wolf, and you will have Javert." Prodded by compulsive retaliation, this petty and merciless police inspector relentlessly pursues Valjean, stalking him at every turn, harassing him at every opportunity, eager to toss him into prison again for any infraction. Incapable of granting compassion, he is also unable to receive it. And when Valjean allows Javert to escape from a situation in which Valjean has the upper hand, this act of kindness and forgiveness is too much for Javert to handle. That, and an uncharacteristic gesture of human understanding toward Valjean, lead him to take his own life. In the Broadway version, Javert despairs before his suicide:

Who is this man?
Vengeance was his and he gave me back my
life. . . . I'll spit his pity right back in his face.

For Valjean, the experience of being forgiven by the bishop opened up new life and led him to sanctity. For Javert, the inability to receive forgiveness and to understand a world ordered not by law but by compassion led him to death.

There is power connected with forgiveness. How we use that power is ours to decide. Either way, the stakes are high.

OBSTACLES TO FORGIVING

There are five common obstacles to forgiveness.

The time commitment. Forgiveness is part of a process that begins with a hurt and ends with the event of reconciliation. To reconcile means to bring together that which belongs together but that is apart. It works only when we become aware of the depths of the offense against us and the anger burning within us, and only when we pause to forgive, so that we can be reconciled with all our wits about us.

Faking forgiveness is common and accomplishes nothing. It simply postpones the eventual confrontation with hurts and resentments that always need to be dealt with and surrendered before healing can happen. The Band-Aid approach is never adequate.

There is no official time line connected with forgiving. Each situation has its own inner timing that cannot be ignored. We need patience to guide us through the healing of emotional, psychological, and spiritual hurts just as we need to be patient when we are being healed of physical wounds.

Only on television do people who have spent a lifetime wounding each other achieve reconciliation within an hour or two. For most mortals, the process is often slower than anticipated. Seldom are the "real life" parties instantaneously in synch with each other: when one is willing to grant forgiveness, the other is not ready to receive it, and vice versa.

Only with God is the timing always perfect, because God is always forgiving. All that remains is the exercise of repentance, which allows us to accept that forgiveness. Human forgiveness, even with God as our model, takes longer to happen and the time involved often frightens away those eager for a quick fix.

The fear of confrontation. The act of forgiveness frequently involves coming into conflict with the one who offended us or who harmed someone we love. The temptation is to wave the flag of capitulation. "Peace at any price" is more attractive than clearly addressing the offender, communicating one's hurts, and working through the pain.

The simpler route *seems* to be forgetting the whole matter, pretending it never happened, hoping it will never happen again. Frequently, anything appears preferable to direct confrontation.

And because of our reluctance, the hurt and the possibility of its forgiveness often do not get the attention they deserve.

Our life experience may be inconsistent with forgiveness.

People whose lives have not included forgiving relationships, especially in the formative childhood years, are severely handicapped in the exercise of forgiveness. We need to have known a friendship sometime in our past that was strong enough to withstand misunderstandings, trials, and upset. Recalling such a relationship shows us the possibility of restoring a fractured relationship in the present: done once, it can be done again.

The exercise of forgiveness depends heavily on a life history that includes the experience of forgiveness. The good news is that even one single friendship that included forgiveness is enough to trigger a new frame of reference and enable us to practice the exercise.

Repentance. The realignment necessary in the act of repentance is the fourth obstacle to the exercise of forgiveness. Repentance requires us to reassess and to readjust our ways of behaving and thinking. If we are the offenders in need of forgiveness from others and from God, repentance urges us to surrender our stubborn hearts and to be humble enough to ask for pardon.

Sincere repentance involves a firm resolve about not repeating the negative behavior and trying to make amends for the injury we caused.

Repentance is a way of returning ourselves to God's dominion and that of our true selves; it extricates us from the dominion of our false selves. It begins with ruthless honesty about who we are and acute self-awareness. The process leads us to profound insight about God's holiness, which stands in direct contrast to our sinfulness. It also reveals something of the depth of God's love for us.

Curiously, a repentant attitude combines the paradoxical strains of grieving and celebrating. We grieve over the loss of our addictions, sins, and offenses to which we have become attached, but we celebrate, too, our freedom from them. The struggle and tears are a foretaste of freedom and joy. But it is never easy to realign one's loyalties and leave the past behind.

Repentance says that hard though it is, it is worth the cost.

Pride. On one side, pride does not allow the offender to seek forgiveness. But on the other side, pride often stands in the way of granting forgiveness, too.

Pride of place or status urges those in authority to demand payment rather than to relent and forgive. The pressure of friends and family to exercise control over the situation prevents people from forgiving those who have offended them. And the need to require punishment is pervasive. Nowhere, perhaps, is this more visible than in our prison system, which prompted Martin Luther King, Jr., to comment: "Go to any prison and ask the inhabitants who have written shameful lines across the pages of their lives. From behind the bars they will tell you that a society is slow to forgive. . . . Jesus eloquently affirmed from the cross a higher law. He knew that the old eye-for-an-eye philosophy would leave everyone blind."

BENEFITS OF FORGIVENESS

Willingness to forgive, long before any single act of forgiveness is complete, brings benefits because it enables a person to participate directly in God's intention for the universe—unity and reconciliation.

Yet the benefits of forgiveness, unlike benefits of other exercises in this book, are often gradual and will be seen most clearly over a long period of time.

Among the most prominent, let me highlight six:

Forgiveness disengages us from internal turmoil. The internal struggle that pushes us toward revenge is yielded with forgiveness. A truce takes place that results in peace and inner security. The knots in the stomach or aches across our shoulders that were symptomatic of the wrenching that took place within us are no longer directing us. Even our bodies feel the tension and stress slipping away. Our spirits are blessed with the same benefits.

Forgiveness lets us trust again. Nonforgiveness sets up barriers in our relationships. Hurt once, we are guarded about being hurt again and we trust warily, if at all. For example, the middle-aged business executive who loses his job because of a power play within the organization may decide not to forgive those who orchestrated his downfall. He will be reluctant to trust new associates at a new firm. Perhaps he will be cautious about trusting *anyone,* preferring instead to shut everyone out of his life.

Forgiveness releases him from that bondage. It allows him to be sensible, of course, about where and to whom he confides, but it does not enclose him in a friendless, solitary world. Forgiveness enables him to let go of the hurt, to learn from it, and to trust again. It allows relationships to exist on more than a superficial plane. It opens up the possibility of intimacy.

Forgiveness is healing. Like a flesh wound that cannot heal when it is continually irritated, the wounds that call for forgiveness do not heal if they are intercepted by negative memories that keep them alive. When forgiveness does not take place, each time we remember the hurt we scratch open the wound. When forgiveness does not take place, the wound is subjected to continuous abuse.

All wounds need to be cleansed before healing can occur. Forgiveness is the process that lets us look at our hurts directly, face the fact that we have been wounded by another's behavior, and then *consciously* and *actively* forgive. After we begin the process of forgiveness, we are able to remember the offense without its controlling our behavior. We are free from the tyranny that the negative deed formerly imposed on us.

Forgiveness frees energy for things other than revenge. No longer obsessed with getting even, no longer totally preoccupied by revenge, we are now free to turn our attention to other interests and to channel energy into other activities.

Nonforgiveness paralyzes us because it demands such total focus.

Forgiveness benefits our relationships. All of our relationships—with others, with ourselves, and with God—suffer when nonforgiveness consumes us. One reason for this is that our preoccupation with the offense against us urges us to incorporate our friends and family in a network of revenge or shunning.

Forgiveness extends beyond us as a way of life. Forgiveness has a ripple effect, happily for us and those in relationships with us.

The greatest benefit of this exercise is that it allows all the other exercises in this book, and many others besides, to happen.

TO EXERCISE FORGIVENESS

The place to begin exercising forgiveness is with ourselves.

1. *Take inventory of places where forgiveness needs to be extended.* If the inventory reveals places in need of healing, we need to think about our readiness to move in the direction of peace. Even if the other party (or parties) is not ready or is unwilling to cooperate with our peace proposal, this may be the right time *for us* to dismantle barriers so that nothing, on our side of things at least, stands in the way of a reconciliation.

We can let it be known by word or gesture that we are willing to declare a new relationship.

2. *Review situations in your life where you may be "faking" reconciliation.* These may be places where you've decided on the "peace-at-any-price" plan of nonaction. Maybe this is the time to re-assess those situations, decide that you will confront the hurt (alone, with a friend, or with the person who offended you) and deal with the pain you are enduring.

3. *Consider those places where someone may be trying to make amends and finds you resistant.* Think about that . . . gently. Are you someone who asks for and expects mercy and forgiveness from others (and God) but is stingy in granting forgiveness and mercy to those around you? If there is an inconsistency in your life in this regard, perhaps you can promise yourself that you will reconsider and declare a lasting truce.

4. *Examine relationships around you—between family members, at work, in the community, in church.* Are you tired of saying about such situations: "Leave them alone . . . they'll work out their own problems"? Can you see yourself as an active peacemaker in any of these settings? Is there something you can do to help communication, confrontation, and eventual reconciliation for persons at odds with each other? Can you see yourself approaching one or more of the persons involved and saying, "I'm aware of the tension and hurt going on in your life. Is there anything I can do to relieve the burden you are experiencing?"

5. *Is there a reconciliation that you have been instrumental in cementing—in your own life or the lives of others?* If so, be grateful for your response, because Jesus said, "Blessed are the peacemakers," and you are one of them. You deserve a little celebrating!

6. *Is God's forgiveness real to you?* If not, consider rereading some stories of the forgiveness of Jesus. The parable of the indulgent son who is welcomed home—no questions asked (Luke 15:11–32) and the story of the repentant sinner at Simon's house (Luke 7:36–49) may be helpful places to begin. They each tell about God's unconditional, no-strings-attached style of forgiveness, where Jesus goes first and does not allow the offense to stand in the way of his relationship with the offender.

These and other episodes in the New Testament are encouraging reading.

7. *Collect stories of those who have forgiven.* The witnessing of people who have forgiven will help when you need to forgive a child's ingratitude, a friend's betrayal, a nation's indifference to the poor. Save the stories of those who have forgiven and read them again and again for strength and motivation.

One place to begin, of course, is the Bible. Jesus on the cross says that those who are responsible "do not know what they are doing."

When Stephen is about to be stoned to death, he prays for his executioners: "Do not hold this sin against them" (Acts 7:60).

Or consider the story of Father Titus Brandsma, a Dutch Carmelite priest arrested by the Nazis in 1942 for advising journalists in his country not to publish press releases from the Nazis. His sentence at Dachau was execution by lethal injection. Father Brandsma told the nurse responsible for the injection that he forgave her and gave her his rosary. That gesture prompted a change of heart, and the nurse eventually told his story even though she could have been tried as a war criminal. At ceremonies for the beatification of Father Brandsma in 1985, the nurse was present as a special guest.

8. *Collect stories of those who have made restitution to others.* The story of Frederick Downs, a former infantry lieutenant in Vietnam in 1967, may be a good place to begin.

In *No Longer Enemies, Not Yet Friends,* Downs tells of returning to Vietnam several times between 1987 and 1989 as part of the Reagan administration's effort to prod the Vietnamese government to account for missing American service personnel.

What he found during his return visits surprised him, and his discoveries catch us off guard, too. Instead of faceless ciphers against whom he had harbored bitter hatred all these years, Downs found men and women who play with their children, care for their aging parents, and work hard for a living in a country so poor that cosmetics are sold by the smear from doorways.

Downs recalled his days as a twenty-three-year-old officer following orders to capture or kill the enemy:

> There were times we had fired into the villages because the enemy was there among the people. . . . I never thought of the villages as anything other than a cluster of meaningless primitive mud and straw huts. I knew people lived in the "hootches," but I never thought of them as homes. I never thought of myself as destroying someone's home.
>
> I did not realize or care that the villages were the history, the guts and the backbone of Vietnam.

Evidently, neither the President of the United States nor the Pentagon thought or cared much about it, either.

Back in the United States, Downs found peace in his work to secure medicine and rehabilitation equipment for Vietnamese survivors of the war. The "knot of politics and history between the two countries would never unravel without attempting to pull a strand. In this case, the strand was humanitarian aid."

As director of prosthetics for the Veteran's Administration, Downs has carved out a niche for himself among a people "no longer enemies, not yet friends." In the process, his story discloses the way one man surrendered prejudice and hatred and discovered his nemesis as a human being like himself.

9. *Be creative about healing your hurts.* When Candy Lightner's daughter was killed by a drunk driver, she used her anger and energy to found Mothers Against Drunk Driving (MADD). The organization works for tougher laws against driving while under the influence of alcohol in an effort to prevent this kind of tragedy from happening again.

Instead of stewing and corroding her inner being with thoughts of vengeance, Lightner pushed that energy into work that helps everyone (even drunk drivers).

10. *Resist the advice of well-meaning people who say that forgiveness is impossible.* It is *always* possible. And people have lived to tell of new lives after they forgave. Husbands and wives who have forgiven unfaithful spouses *have* been reconciled to each other after forgiveness. Children abused by their parents *have* forgiven the cruelty and have been healed of tragic hurts.

The invitation not to forgive is frequently an invitation to remain resentful and hating, sometimes for a lifetime.

Forgiveness offers another alternative, and the benefits are awesome for the forgiver. Forgiveness says that the decisions of life, even when they turn out badly, are not beyond repair. And hope. And peace.

Who could ask for more than that?

NOTES

The epigraph comes from Dag Hammarskjöld, *Markings* (New York: Knopf, 1977), 124.

See William Klassen's book *The Forgiving Community* (Philadelphia: Westminster Press, 1966) for an overview of the biblical understanding of forgiveness. See also C.F.D. Moule, "The Christian Understanding of Forgiveness," in *From Fear to Faith: Studies of Suffering and Wholeness* (London: S.P.C.K., 1971), 61–72. Moule's point is that there is no room for retribution in the Christian understanding of forgiveness.

On the subject of "owning" and "disowning," see A. Angyal, "The Convergence of Psychotherapy and Religion," *Journal of Pastoral Care*, 5, (1952), 4–14.

Reporting on the Terry Anderson story, "Delivered from Hell," by Nancy Gibbs, comes from *Time*, December 16, 1991, 16–17.

James N. Lapsley approaches the canceled debt theme from a perspective different from mine. See his article "Reconciliation, Forgiveness, Lost Contracts" in *Theology Today* 23 (April 1966), 45–59.

Nathaniel Hawthorne's *Scarlet Letter* (originally published 1850) is still a classic story on the complexities of forgiveness and the double standard employed in some cases.

New Testament approaches to forgiveness are part of a study I completed called "Forgiveness and Recidivism," in *Pastoral Psychology* 33 (Fall 1984), 15–24. Especially helpful to me were the following: F. W. Beare, *The Gospel According to Matthew* (Oxford: Basil Blackwell, 1981); R. H. Gundry, *Matthew: A Commentary on His Literary and Theological Art* (Grand Rapids, MI: Eerdmans, 1982); C. J. Roetzel, *Judgment in the Community* (Leiden: E. J. Brill, 1972); Richard Kugelman, C. P., "The First Letter to the Corinthians," in *Jerome Biblical Commentary* (Englewood, Cliffs, NJ: Prentice-Hall, 1968); and J. P. Meyer, *Ministers of Christ: A Commentary on the Second Epistle of Paul to the Corinthians* (Milwaukee, WI: Northwestern Publishing House, 1963).

A valuable study of revenge and its place vis-à-vis forgiveness is offered by Susan Jacoby, *Wild Justice: The Evolution of Revenge* (New York: Harper & Row, 1983).

Martin Luther King, Jr., "Loving Our Enemies," in *Strength to Love* (New York: Collins Fount paperback, 1969), 47–55, is the source for Dr. King's comments on enemies.

For the quotations from Victor Hugo's novel *Les Misérables* (New York: Signet, 1987), see 106 for the bishop's transaction with Valjean and 170 for the comparison of Javert to a wolf.

The lyrics quoted come from *Les Misérables*, a musical by Alain Boublil and Claude-Michel Schonberg, based on the novel by Victor Hugo; music by Claude-Michel Schonberg, lyrics by Herbert Kretzmer.

The source for the Martin Luther King, Jr., quote on prison and forgiveness is his essay "Love in Action," in *Strength to Love* (New York: Collins Fount Paperback, 1969), 39.

For Father Brandsma's story, see the *Christopher News Notes*, No. 347, July/August 1992, called "The Power of Forgiveness." The Christophers (12 E. 48 St., NY, NY 10017) regularly publish stories of men and women whose actions show that "it is better to light one candle than to curse the darkness."

See Frederick Downs, *No Longer Enemies, Not Yet Friends* (New York: Norton, 1991), 262.

For Candy Lightner's story see "Original Thinkers: These Five Helped Reshape the Way We See Our World—And Live In It," in *Life*, Fall 1989, 167.

Chapter 8

PERSEVERING

Let us run with perseverance the race that is set before us.
HEBREWS 12:1

Perseverance wears many faces. One of them belongs to the former San Francisco Giants baseball player Dave Dravecky. Shortly after Dravecky signed with the team, specialists at The Cleveland Clinic diagnosed cancer in his pitching arm. Doctors were sure of only one thing: "Outside of a miracle, you'll never pitch again." But Dravecky took on an agonizing schedule of physical therapy and rehabilitation, and nine months after an operation that removed half of his deltoid muscle, he was at the mound again.

Dravecky exudes perseverance from every pore of his being. Perseverance comes into play for any of us when the chips are down, when the prognosis is bleak, when our strength is depleted, and a voice from our gut urges us to push on. And we do. Why we don't quit and throw in the towel is a mystery to us. We find that adversity brings out something in us we didn't know we had. Or we see something in friends or relatives we didn't know *they* had. Either way, we are caught off guard by an amazing surge of courage that stares down defeat and says, "I'll make it through this. By God, I will."

But we need not be caught off guard. Adversity isn't the only way to produce perseverance. We can cultivate perseverance by practicing the exercises in this chapter to strengthen our character and our ability to respond to the trials of everyday life, not just the moments of crisis.

For Dravecky, perseverance was part of a longer haul. While pitching in Montreal two months after his comeback, his humerus bone snapped. "The sound was audible all over the field," he wrote. "It sounded as though someone had snapped a heavy tree branch. I felt as though my arm had separated from my body and was sailing off toward home plate . . . I was grabbing my arm to keep it from flying away." Then the cancer reappeared, and another bone in the damaged arm was broken in a freak accident. The second operation was more serious than the first; his left arm and shoulder were amputated.

His baseball career was over now, but Dravecky was certain another path lay before him. In a television interview, the handsome, plainspoken Dravecky put it this way: "I intend to get all I can out of life. I plan to play golf and tennis and swim . . . to hug my family and to live life to the fullest. I think I'm a lucky man."

He wasn't grandstanding. It wasn't pride, or vanity, or showing off on Dravecky's part. We detect in his story honesty and humility, bona fide signals of true perseverance.

Honesty is needed to assess the situation without playing with the facts or denying what is. Humility is the grace to face our own createdness with dignity and to count on another power to carry us through the darkness. It's a team effort. At its best, humility is an active faith: God never said it would be easy, only that God would not abandon us. "God is faithful, and . . . will not let you be tested beyond your strength, but with the testing . . . will also provide the way out so that you may be able to endure it" (1 Cor 10:13). That promise enables us to walk the mile we thought we would not have the strength to travel alone.

In his novel *Till We Have Faces,* C. S. Lewis observed that there are two responses to difficulties: the brittle approach and the flexible one. To stand firm or to bend. Dave Dravecky fuses the two—he is at once hard, tough, enduring, and amazingly flexible when it comes to options for his future.

WAITING FOR THE RAINS TO COME

If flexibility is a clue to perseverance, Jill Ker Conway's mother measures up as another survivor. M.I.T. scholar and former president of Smith College, Jill Ker Conway writes about her mother in the critically acclaimed book *The Road from Coorain*. Mrs. Ker and her husband sink all their money into a sheep and cattle ranch in the Australian outback and watch the ranch prosper until the drought of 1944. With no water, the animals die. The few remaining ones are shot to end their misery. The death of Mr. Ker forces his widow to decide whether to sell the ranch. In spite of blunt advice from bankers and personal battles with depression, she holds on to it until the rains come. She leaves Coorain and hopes for the chance to return and start all over again.

Resettled in Sydney, with ranch-sitters guarding the 18,000 decimated acres at Coorain, she holds down two jobs to raise her family as a single parent. She also devises a plan.

Estimating that sheep prices will soar when rain comes, she decides that she will make her sheep purchases when rain is spotted as far as 300 miles away. With flawless business instincts, she watches the news reports, borrows funds, and signs a deal for ewes. In a matter of hours, her investment doubles when her gamble proves right. When the rains come, her calculated risk propels the family into a life of financial security.

Mrs. Ker is a clear case study of perseverance—the ability to stick by her plans despite the constant reminders that it is potential folly, that she should behave as women are supposed to behave, acquiescent and docile. Instead, whatever obstacle emerges, she turns another corner around it.

Resiliency is crucial to perseverance. As a teacher, I have watched it come into play over and over again. Not long ago a premed student I knew got a C in anatomy. She intensified her effort, tried over again in summer school, succeeded, and eventually went on to medical school. During the same semester another premed student also got a

C in anatomy. This student did some realistic soul-searching about his aptitude for medicine and chose another field, confident that in the process he hadn't lost but won. Both students were, each in his or her own way, resilient.

THE WAY DOWN IS UP

While some people like Mrs. Ker exercise at least partial (and sometimes successful) control over the externals of their destiny, there are others who are totally deprived of that opportunity. The stories of Nelson Mandela, Andrei Sakharov, Viktor Frankl, and Irina Ratushinskaya bear this out. What these (and many less famous) men and women do is remind us that even when determining outside conditions is out of the question, an inner determination is possible. These people stand witness to an inner attitude of perseverance, even when the outer conditions appear hopeless.

Nobel laureate Alexander Solzhenitsyn introduces us in virtually all of his novels to characters who survive against the most extraordinary odds. Under the most deprived and depraved conditions, one by one, his characters manage not only to persevere but to persevere intact.

Driven to the brink of despair under conditions specifically devised to snuff out life and a person's spirit, Shukhov, the hero of *One Day in the Life of Ivan Denisovich,* maintains a dignity that transcends his grimy, sordid, inhumane surroundings. Though it would seem from the outside that every ounce of hope has been squeezed out of the inmates of Stalin's prison system, Shukhov's presence says no, it is not so. It is possible, he says, to live on in this squalid dump not as an animal but as a human with feelings, dignity, and principles.

What kind of feelings, dignity, and principles? Feelings of joy—for example, when Shukhov eats his soup and jubilantly discovers a piece of fish in it, or when it is hot and "courses down through his body," as he savors each sensation. At times like these his perseverance is strengthened and he reinforces his belief: "We'll survive. We'll stick it out, God willing, till it's over." In this God-forsaken place, it is possible to find an occasionally happy and decent human being. Shukhov is one. He does kindnesses for others, will not take advantage of others, will not inform on others, and will not ask favors if by asking them he becomes beholden to the system.

Shukhov is a moral man in an immoral society. He refuses to sell out to the authorities even if it means privileges for himself; he has principles and a tireless wish to keep a living soul in a living body.

Shukhov is not deluded. He transfers the discovery he has made about his own humanity on to others, believing that there are others who are decent people, too. Anne Frank also discovered that. Despite her suffering she wrote, "I still believe that people are good at heart."

In a perverted way, even in the prisons of the Gulag, or Dachau, or South Africa, or Central America, some persons *could* control at least part of their external destinies. All these few needed was to turn in a friend, or lie, and they would have it made. Solzhenitsyn's characters tell us what's at stake in such a deal: selling one's soul and then living with one's empty self.

No matter what the personal advantage, some of Solzhenitsyn's characters simply cannot cave in. Nerzhin, for example, the central character in *The First Circle,* is sent to a prison for scientists where there is meat and butter and hot water. The price for these luxuries is to cooperate with the regime. The options are spelled out clearly for him: remain in these comfortable, cushioned surroundings or risk starvation, torture, or death in a typical prison. Not only does Nerzhin choose the less privileged place, but he also feels more at home there. Stripped of everything, he finds that only under such conditions can he be at peace with himself and his principles. Call it integrity, character, moral force. Whatever its name, it is a choice that enables Nerzhin to bottom out rather than to sell out, and to find in the depths of his will the capacity to undergo a spiritual growth and purification that is redemptive. Nerzhin is convinced (and convinces us) that only by living through hell can he experience paradise.

SYMBOLS OF PERSEVERANCE

The story of Václav Havel, the former president of Czechoslova-kia, parallels these insights from Solzhenitsyn. As far back as 1948 when the Communists took power and his family landholdings were confiscated, Havel was part of a defiant underground. When the Soviets marched into Prague in 1968, Havel knew he had to stay and wait and do what he could to form a coalition that would gather strength and be ready to take over when the time was right. Convinced that it was worth persevering, committed to the emancipation of his homeland, and unlike other dissidents who fled, Havel spoke boldly and wrote defiantly until he was put under surveillance and jailed.

When several U.S. senators met with Havel in Czechoslovakia in 1970, they told him what they thought was good news. They intended to press for legislation that would allow dissidents like Havel to emigrate to the West.

Havel replied that he was not interested in going to the West. "What good would that do?" he asked. "Only by staying here and struggling here can we ever hope to change things."

Havel and Solzhenitsyn speak the same truth about perseverance: sometimes there is no choice but to stay faithful. When the cause draws followers, it speaks to the same desire for freedom in them. The cause is not simply popular but true to the human spirit.

In 1980, in a destitute and dilapidated Haiti, a tenacious and resilient thirty-seven-year-old priest came on the scene. The savage military force from the Duvalier regime known as the Tontons Macoute were back in force and 91% of the people lived below the poverty level. Jean-Bertrand Aristide breathed hope into the hearts of the people. He worked with beggars and homeless and the largely unemployed urban youth of a harsh city of well over a million people. As Aristide's following grew, so did threats on his life. There was pressure from the government and the church to transfer him, but when the plans became known, the youth of Port-au-Prince began a hunger strike. The transfer was rescinded.

After the hunger strike, a paid assassin was foiled in his attempt to kill Aristide. He survived several other attempts on his life, including a car ambush. When the Salesians, the Roman Catholic order of priests to which he belonged, expelled him from the order, Aristide kept a low profile for a while but reappeared when the message "Pale, Sikile," ("Speak, move among us") was sprayed on buildings throughout the capital. Deprived of a pulpit, he found that the country became his parish—and his voice was amplified through an underground that looked to him as a prophet.

Aristide was elected president of Haiti on December 16, 1990. A coup on January 8, 1991, attempted to wrest the power from Aristide and the poor, but on February 7, 1991, amid widespread jubilation among the poor, he was inaugurated to do the most difficult job in the American hemisphere where the average life expectancy is fifty and one child dies every five minutes of disease and malnutrition.

Even after a coup on September 30, 1991, ousted Aristide from office, the perseverance of Aristide and the poor continues.

Whatever the final outcome in Czechoslovakia or in Haiti, the people have turned Havel and Aristide into symbols of perseverance capable of creating a new politics and generating new social structures. The symbols evoke passionate desire and give new vision and energy that refuses to be conquered.

WHEN MELTDOWN HAPPENS

Many stories about perseverance are related to depression. It is often the case that the troubles we face—the *reasons* we are called on to persevere—spiral us near the brink of despair. A marriage falls apart, or a loved one dies or is imprisoned; we lose a job, or a promotion, or a friendship. Sometimes we can pinpoint none of these losses, yet slowly a depression comes over us. We struggle to overcome it, and most often we do, but that is of little consolation when we are in the thick of it.

At the turn of the century, Elizabeth Bayley Seton, a member of New York Episcopalian society, converted to Roman Catholicism. A widow with five children, she was disowned by her family and treated with suspicion by Episcopalians and Roman Catholics alike. Yet she persevered and eventually obtained the permission needed to found the Sisters of Charity, pioneers in both health care and Catholic education in the United States.

Mother Seton knew some low points in her life, but the lowest of them all was when her sixteen-year-old daughter Anna Maria died.

Elizabeth Seton wrote: "After Nina was taken I was so often expecting to lose my senses and my head was so disordered that unless for the daily duties always before me I did not know much of what I did or what I left undone." Although two daughters and two sons were still alive and her religious community offered support through her ordeal, Mother Seton's anguish was so profound that some of those closest to her thought she might not emerge from her grief. Writing to a friend she said, "The separation from my angel has left so new and deep an impression on my mind, that if I was not obliged to live in these dear ones I should unconsciously die in her."

Stories like this remind us that depression is a human experience that happens to all kinds of people—secretaries and senators, bishops and bus drivers, and even to Roman Catholic widows who become leaders of religious communities. Although some people have a harder time than others getting through the hassles of life, depression/despair can strike anyone. Sometimes all one can do is live through its pain and suffering in order to come out on the other side, even when the thought of surviving seems remote.

Depression chokes the will to persevere. American novelist William Styron captures the pathos of this in the extraordinary personal glimpse he provides of the time he felt "the wind of the wing of madness"—to borrow a phrase from the French poet Baudelaire. In Connecticut, at his "beloved home for thirty years"—the one place in the world that teemed with security, warmth, and fond memories—despair crept into and clutched his heart. On a walk one day, he noticed a flight of birds. "Ordinarily, I would have been exhilarated"; instead, gripped by depression, he shivered stranded and helpless. "Depression" does not seem to be an accurate word for what he lived through: "storm of murk," "brainstorm," and "meltdown" are Styron's alternatives. He records their effects: slowed-down responses, near-paralysis, psychic energy close to zero, exhaustion, despair, and thoughts of death. This is precisely the impact of depression—it disables a person to the point of no return, first mocking and then destroying any effort to carry on.

The mother of one of my son's classmates once confided to me that she was so depressed that she did not think she could make it through the school year. To the casual observer, the woman had everything to live for—every imaginable material comfort, a devoted husband, four wonderful children, and a productive career, but depression forces its victim to read the evidence differently. "I cannot survive another October," she told me. "I die with every leaf, every flower."

Depression vitiates the will to persevere. Face-to-face with depression, even the giants among us knuckle under. The question then becomes how to persevere through depression and how to make it through the tunnel to the light.

"WE LIVE BY HOPE" (ST. PAUL)

Hope imagines what has not yet happened but still is possible. One of the most credible guides to finding the light of hope in the darkness is William Lynch. A Jesuit priest, Father Lynch was once described as "someone who cherishes the presence of hope because he knows the anguish of its loss." He offers four important clues to survive through depression: hoping, wishing, friendship, and waiting.

To hope, according to Lynch, is to acknowledge three basic ideas: (1) What I hope for I do not have and cannot see; (2) It may be difficult; (3) I *can* have it. It is possible *for me* to hope.

This sounds to me like what Nelson Mandela did in Africa, what Shukhov did in Soviet Russia under Stalin, what Jean-Bertrand Aristide did in Haiti, what Elizabeth Bayley Seton did in New York and Maryland, what Dave Dravecky did in San Francisco, and what William Styron did in Connecticut. Father Lynch hurries to point out that the kind of hope he means is not the popular romantic image in which hopelessness is disguised as hope. This happens routinely when people use expressions like "Well, there's nothing left for us to do but hope," which in translation means "We might as well give up. It's hopeless." Instead, the hope that Lynch writes about comes straight from the Gospels of the New Testament and the letters of the Apostle Paul. This kind of hope defies logic, but hangs on to the promises of Jesus. Without being able to see it, we press for a future of glory and know with certitude that, in some form, a resurrection will come.

The wishing Lynch speaks of is not romantic either. Nor is it escapism, but rather the way the imagination exercises itself to find a way out of the predicament. Consider a woman who has been in a battering relationship for fifteen years. Her situation seems hopeless. She judges that she cannot leave the abusive relationship because she has nowhere to go. She wishes it were otherwise (and Lynch would see even this fragile wishing as a sign of life!), but she has no job skills and no money. She also has the children to think about, and she is sure that the abuser will track her down no matter where she hides.

Her tentative wishing is helped along the way by people who create, organize, and administer protective shelters for such women. Lynch has this kind of activity in mind when he speaks of friendship. Friendship says we do not have to strike against despair all by ourselves because there is someone wishing along with us. "Wishing with" bolsters the hope of the one on the line.

In his darkest hour, William Styron bore out Lynch's thesis. Styron tells of the daily phone calls he received from a newspaper columnist who had just survived a bout with suicidal depression himself. The passionate, committed support of this person was a priceless lifeline, persuading Styron of life's worth, convincing him that the illness would run its course and that suicide was unacceptable. The caller graciously (and no doubt honestly) told Styron that the help he gave Styron "had been a continuing therapy for him."

If the antidote to despair involves hoping, wishing, and friendship, it also involves waiting. At rock bottom, perseverance asks that we cope with obstacles, remain fixed on a goal, and that we stand poised, ready to spring if an opportunity presents itself. "The positive waiting of hope," writes Lynch, "has made up its mind and wishes so strongly that it will wait for what it wants."

REVOLUTIONARY PATIENCE

We could test Lynch's observations further by taking a look at Celie's life, as Alice Walker presents this character to us in her novel *The Color Purple*.

Celie's situation is abysmal. Raped by the man who claims to be her father, she bears him two children who are taken from her. Abused by her husband and her mean-spirited stepchildren, she is virtually a slave in her own home. Even so, Celie never gives up hope although only a faint glimmer burns in her soul.

It is only when a friend, Shug Avery, enters Celie's life that the spark of hope is fanned. Lynch would say that hope grows because Celie has someone who shares her wishing. Shug and other women even prod Celie to wish more than she does. "You deserve more than this," one of them says to her. And when Celie protests, Shug insists and encourages Celie to wait patiently for the time she can leave her husband and follow her dream of being a seamstress. All of this, eventually, comes to be. Hoping, wishing, friendship, and waiting move Celie from hopelessness and despair to a creative future, not by magic but by persevering at each juncture in the process. It happens by living through the pain, by guarding with one's very life the tiny light of hope, by finding and treasuring unselfish support wherever we find it—and what a ministry this is!—and by waiting for the new day to dawn.

Patience is very much part of the process. Perseverance and patience are virtually synonymous. It is one thing to be called on to do something virtuous occasionally—almost anyone can muster the strength and courage for that. But patience asks that we overcome the fatigue that invites us to quit; it asks us to persist in a course of action for a long time.

While patience is involved in perseverance, it is not a weak and passive patience. The virtue of patience—as opposed to the caricature of patience—is an active exercise of power. It is worth cultivating because it enables us to continue efforts despite obstacles, delays, or the temptation to quit; to act strongly without complaint, to believe in the future, and to keep on keeping on.

"GOD IS DEEF, I RECKON." (CELIE)

The waiting that Celie does, and that we do in our turn, is also a waiting for God. It seems as though even God has disappeared when we need divine aid the most. Celie puts it this way:

> What God do for me? I ast.... He give me a
> lynched daddy, a crazy mama, a lowdown dog of a
> step pa and a sister I probably won't ever see again....
> All my life I never care what people thought bout
> nothing I did, I say. But deep in my heart I care about
> God. What he going to think. And come to find out,
> he don't think. Just sit up there glorying in being
> deef, I reckon. But it ain't easy, trying to do without
> God. Even if you know he ain't there, trying to do
> without him is a strain.

Religious language calls this the dark night. Characterized by powerlessness, disappointment, loss of meaning, and helplessness, the dark night eclipses the brightness we thought we possessed forever. When we turn for support, all the old familiar faces are gone and we sense betrayal. The familiar ways of doing things and the ways we found helpful in the past also elude us. Nothing eases the pain and loneliness. Celie is right in her assessment: "God *is* deef," or at least this is our experience of God. We are, it seems, totally alone.

For St. John of the Cross, who perhaps more than anyone else is associated with the concept and symbolism of the dark night, this was a time of opportunity, growth, and productivity. The dark night is truly a sign of life but is experienced as death. So we panic and try to control what resists our management; and in fact, John of the Cross was careful to advise that the more we do to extricate ourselves from this night, the worse it gets.

To understand the symbolism of the dark night in John of the Cross's terms we must be aware of our *desires*. We are a mixed bag of motives and desires, and the night unveils our need for satisfaction and pleasure to keep us going in relationships. John points out that even in prayer our faithfulness is connected with affective responses. We seem to need to know that God is listening and loving us. So the challenge of the night, according to Constance FitzGerald, is "to make the passage from loving, serving, [and] being with [someone] because of the pleasure and joy it gives us, to loving and serving regardless of the cost." "Darkness," she goes on to say, "is where egoism dies, and true, unselfish love is set free."

What is at stake is not that our desires are crushed, but that they are transformed. When the honeymoon stage of a marriage, a friendship, and/or one's relationship with God is over, the possibility of a quieter, deeper, freer, more committed love begins. The choice frames itself this way: to cling to a relationship that has been manipulative, selfish, possessive, and unfree, or to unclasp our hold and let the other be who and what they are, experience the real potential of the dark night, and be energized to live.

"80 PERCENT OF LIFE IS SHOWING UP" (WOODY ALLEN)

Understanding the dark night is especially pertinent to exercising perseverance, because in this radical experience of abandonment when the heaviness of disappointment weighs us down, John of the Cross calls on us to wait. To struggle our way out will be counterproductive. To attempt to control the situation is impossible because we are no longer in charge. We wait because there is nothing else we can do. As we wait we must grieve over what we are losing when we surrender our possessive and jealous ways of loving. We wait with faith that God will rescue us, eventually, on terms other than our own.

John of the Cross encourages us to live through the waiting and not to run from it. For John of the Cross, faith is exercised every time we wake up and face the new day, for in the waking we remain faithful. Woody Allen contemporizes this insight when he says that "80% of life is showing up."

And maybe most important of all, the experience of the dark night offers the secret of endurance—that God exists even when God is invisible. Glimpses of the hidden God may be present when we look with faith. The hidden God is active, alive, not separate from our world. We can find God as we read the newspaper, play with a child, or work.

It helps to know that the hidden God became visible to us through Jesus. Jesus persevered through daily frustrations, fatigue, and disappointments, even when it seemed that God had abandoned him. Jesus lived among people who misunderstood, misjudged, and betrayed him. He lived out perseverance in the spirit and the flesh.

It takes perseverance to uncover this God. It takes a special kind of faith, too, the kind that endures, keeping in mind that the one who endures to the end will be saved (Mark 13:13).

THE PERSEVERANCE OF THE SAINTS

Perseverance is not stoicism. We must experience both the difficulty of our struggle and the promise of Jesus that he would be with us. The Christian knows that the Apostle Paul was right when he said, "I can do all things through Christ who sustains me."

Paul likewise knew the danger of enthusiasm in conversions. Perseverance asks that we take the longer view. It does not depend on excitement or danger or novelty to keep it alive. The New Testament encourages us all to stay the course. And when the writer to the Hebrews singles out Moses as an example of the kind of faith he commends to us, he doesn't speak of the parting of the Red Sea or of the burning bush. Instead, he sums up Moses's virtue in two words: "He persevered" (Heb. 11:27).

Many saints since the time of Moses and Jesus have done the same. The stories of other people—Celie and Shukhov, for example—are passed down to us through literature. We find examples in our families, good people who manage to cope and push on even when their energy and will are sapped. All of these people are signs or sacraments, because they disclose something of the reality of God, a God whose word perseveres (Isa. 40:8) and whose mercy endures forever (Lam. 3:22). We are in very good company, with God and the saints, when we exercise perseverance.

OBSTACLES TO PERSEVERANCE

The obstacles to perseverance have been highlighted throughout this text, but in summary they are as follows:

Depression is the major obstacle to perseverance because it tempts us, as no other force does, to give up. Depression suffocates the will to go on. While there is no way to avoid depression, there are ways to manage it. William Lynch suggests hoping, wishing, friendship, and waiting as healthy antidotes. Remaining faithful while waiting may not seem like much, but it is at the heart of perseverance.

The habit of being pampered limits our capacity to persevere. Perseverance requires a toughness that stares at adversity head-on and faces the odds without blinking. When we are cushioned from the world's blows, small or large, our endurance ability evaporates.

Self-pity allows us to interiorize the identity of a victim. An inner tape that plays messages like "This is unfair" and "You don't deserve this" invites us to sulk and feel sorry for ourselves. These attitudes oppose those required for perseverance. After disappointment, the one who sulks is content soaking her feet all day in Epsom salts; the one who perseveres dusts off her feet, puts on her shoes, and keeps walking.

Stress disables us when it comes to perseverance. Stress distorts reality, increases the pressure, and urges us to resolve crises as quickly as possible even when our best interests might be compromised. Stress forces us to take the short-term view of a situation and to capitulate.

Fatigue is closely connected with stress. Fatigue clouds our ability to see clearly to make appropriate decisions. Fatigue disfigures our judgment and convinces us that perseverance is impossible.

These are two very dangerous elements—stress and fatigue—and not to be underestimated in the harm they can do. When the body is under pressure, it fails to muster the energy needed to see us through, even when the mind and spirit see the value of bringing something to completion.

Stress and fatigue are also dangerous because they undermine the self-possession we need to make the hard choices—to see through the difficulties and hardship and to emerge wounded, perhaps, but with our integrity intact.

TO EXERCISE PERSEVERANCE

1. *Take one step at a time and follow through at each stage in the course of perseverance.* We are more easily tempted to quit when we try to tackle a whole project all at once. To deal with too many days or

projects is debilitating. "Today's trouble is enough for today" (Matt. 6:34) is a helpful piece of wisdom to keep in mind.

2. *Avoid flashy starts and poor finishes.* Putting all of our energy into the beginning of our work or play is ultimately counterproductive if we can't make it to the finish line. The tortoise proved that slow and steady wins the race.

3. *Keep things in perspective.* Keep mountains and molehills separate. If you need help gaining perspective ask for it. So much of perseverance has to do with seeing the task, trouble, or disappointment clearly and realistically. Perspective is not only necessary, it is crucial.

4. *Recognize the difference between optimism and hope.* Optimism is a positive attitude; hope is a virtue.

Optimism is a mindset that sees what is positive. It is a belief that there is something positive in every situation.

Hope, on the other hand, is based on a vision or religious belief that no matter how reality presents itself, all shall be well and that someday, somewhere, there will be a resurrection.

Hope, then, is far stronger than optimism because it is based on something deeper in the human soul.

5. *Cultivate the discipline of delayed gratification.* There is little in our culture to support this, but perseverance always forgoes immediate pleasure and satisfaction in favor of the long haul.

6. *Cultivate the gift of patience.* Weak, passive, impatient types have a hard time handling glitches and interruptions in plans. They cave in, resort to temper tantrums, blame others, and give up.

7. *Exercise perseverance in conjunction with any or all of the exercises in this book.* For example, if you identify some need for improvement as an affirmer, map out a realistic plan for yourself and stick with it. If your agenda calls for a change of lifestyle with regard to the way you are managing food, plot your course with patience.

8. *Keep a diary of times when you persevered.* A track record in this area, however small, will help build confidence when the next hurdle confronts us.

9. *Cultivate supportive friends.* There is no substitute for the encouragement of friends. *Believe that!*

10. *Learn to recognize the invisible God by learning God's story in Jesus.* Jesus has the power to fill our weakness with God's strength. Perseverance, then, is not an independent activity. It relies on God for its source.

Jesus persevered. So can you with his help.

NOTES

The Dave Dravecky story is based on his book (with Tim Stafford) called *Comeback* (New York: Harper paperbacks, 1990), and on a July 15, 1991, ESPN interview. William Nack's story in *Sports Illustrated,* "Let's Make the Best of It," July 22, 1991, 34–37, was helpful background reading.

The quotation from C. S. Lewis about two responses to difficulties can be found in *Till We Have Faces* (New York: Harcourt, Brace & Co., 1956), 261.

The story of Jill Ker Conway's mother is found in Conway's memoir, *The Road from Coorain* (New York: Vintage Books, 1990); see especially pages 53–119.

Irina Ratushinskaya tells her story in *Grey Is the Color of Hope,* translated by Alyona Kojevnikov (New York: Knopf, 1988).

Terrence Des Pres is the source of the Solzhenitsyn analysis. See his "The Heroism of Survival," in *Aleksandr Solzhenitsyn: Critical Essays and Documentary Materials,* edited by John B. Dunlap *et al.* (Belmont, MA: Nordland, 1973). See also Alexander Solzhenitsyn, *One Day in the Life of Ivan Denisovich,* translated by R. Parker (London: Victor Gollancz, Ltd., 1963), 161.

The story of Nerzhin is found in Alexander Solzhenitsyn, *The First Circle* (New York: Harper & Row, 1968).

Malcolm S. Forbes, Jr., wrote of Václav Havel under the headline "Profile in Courage" in the "Fact and Comment" section of *Forbes,* April 2, 1990, 2.

The information concerning Haiti is quoted from *Comment: Haiti,* by the Catholic Institute for International Relations, 1989. The World Bank called conditions there "beneath any reasonable definition of human decency." For background information on Haiti and Jean-Bertrand Aristide, I relied on Paul Farmer, "The Power of the Poor in Haiti," in *America*, March 19, 1991, 260–267.

The information on Elizabeth Bayley Seton can be found in *Elizabeth Seton: Selected Writings,* edited by Ellin Kelly and Annabelle Melville (Mahwah, NJ: Paulist Press, 1987), 35–36.

William Styron's *Darkness Visible: A Memoir of Madness* (New York: Random House, 1990) is the story of his experience of depression. This extraordinary testimony is required reading.

Images of Hope (Baltimore: Helicon Press, 1965) by William Lynch, S.J., is an excellent guide through depression to hope. It is highly recommended and although out of print, it is worth the effort to acquire it.

Alice Walker, *The Color Purple* (New York: Harcourt Brace Jovanovich, 1982), 164, is the location of Celie's quotation. For reflections on her endurance, see especially 20, 177–184.

For *The Dark Night of St. John of the Cross,* see *The Collected Works of St. John of the Cross,* translated by Kieran Kavanagh and Otillo Rodriguez (Washington, DC: ICS, 1973).

An important essay by Constance FitzGerald, O.C.D., "Impasse and Dark Night," in *Women's Spirituality,* edited by Joann Wolski Conn (Mahwah, NJ: Paulist Press), 287–311, provided insight about John of the Cross, desire, and Alice Walker.

JUST DOING IT

Whenever I feel the urge to take some exercise,
I sit down until the urge passes off.
MARK TWAIN

Human nature being what it is, Mark Twain's comment could apply to spiritual exercises just as easily as to physical ones. Excuses are plentiful for not doing both.

The most popular reasons to avoid exercising are the following:

No time. The day, the week, the month already appear to be too crammed to add a program of spiritual fitness. Yet, we all know there is always time for what we want, what we value, and what we love.

We need to begin slowly. That means: be patient, move at your own pace, and listen. God actually does speak—through events, but especially through other people. Getting in shape spiritually is less like adding something extra to life and more like discovering something already there, waiting to be explored.

Not yet. This is a variation on the "no time" theme. Procrastination tells us there will always be time . . . mañana.

If we wait for the perfect time, we will never begin. Saint Augustine calls this conflict "the agony of indecision." He writes poignantly about this dilemma: "I was held back by mere trifles, the most paltry inanities, all my old attachments." Augustine commiserates with our reluctance, but he also challenges the procrastinator in himself and in us: "In my misery I kept crying, 'How long shall I go on saying "tomorrow, tomorrow"'? Why not now?"

Why not?

Fear of the unknown. Albert Schweitzer prayed, and the next thing he knew he was on his way to Africa. What will happen to us when we make a serious commitment to develop our spiritual lives?

What happens is never more (or less) than what we consent to fully. Our personal freedom is not only preserved but also enhanced when we improve our relationship with God.

No equipment. Books, seminars, or even a degree in theology or divinity is not necessary and may, in fact, stand in the way. All that is needed is the will to begin and to be faithful.

No need. Often we do not see that we need spiritual exercises. Others are far more out of shape than we are. So we are lulled into complacency until a crisis occurs—a loss, a major decision, a failure. Then we discover we are not as fit as we thought.

If we are satisfied with things as they are and have no wish to deepen our lives, we can begin by praying for the desire to pray. That starting point asks God to break through our complacency and to create in us the yearning for things of the spirit.

God unfailingly responds.

The pain. Though the Spirit invites and does not force, spiritual exercise will take its toll.

We need to be careful and practice moderation. The "no pain, no gain" formula can lead to problems. Pain may also indicate that something is not right and that we need to stop pushing ourselves. But no matter how modest the exercise, there will be some minimal discomfort until we hit our stride. Then the resulting exhilaration and joy should more than compensate for the fatigue and pain.

Too late in life. It is never too late to begin exercising the spirit. Some people believe that prayer not cultivated since childhood has no place in midlife or later-life agendas. They think the opportunity for living spirituality has regrettably passed them by.

It is never too late to begin, and there may even be some advantage to a spiritual journey that begins in our more mature years when we experience a deeper need for meaning and for God.

The bottom line is that we maintain a realistic program. Balance is the key. A common mistake among beginners is to overdose or to do unnecessary exercises. When the Spirit is at work, balance—in the exercises themselves and in the results of the exercises —is evident: workaholics acquire playfulness; the lazy get down to work; the serious laugh; and the self-centered reach out to others.

The call to exercise is not an invitation to obey a program but an invitation to love. Exercises are always measured by this simple test: do they lead us to love more courageously and live more justly?

We need to experiment. The exercises in this book are merely suggestions; there are others we may discover once we embark on a journey of spiritual fitness. Some are more suitable for novices and some for those already in shape. Consider other exercises like trusting, desiring, reading, writing, playing, winning, and losing.

We also need to monitor the effects of our exercises, preferably with a companion who has been on this journey before us. The danger signs to watch for are overextension, fatigue, self-absorption, self-complacency, self-righteousness, depression, and the disappointment that we are not measuring up to our own exacting standards. The signs of health (or growth) are those found in Paul's letter to the Galatians, Chapter 5: peace, joy, kindness, love, gentleness, faithfulness, and goodness. When the exercises produce these, we discover a glimpse of the truth that what we love ardently determines what we become.

Notes

For the Augustine quotation on procrastination, see St. Augustine, *The Confessions,* Book 8, Chapter 12 (New York: Penguin Books, 1966).

INDEX

Adams, Doug, 115, 125
Addeo, Edmond G., 17
Aigner, Frederick, 62
Aikido, 123–24
Amnesty International, 92, 107, 109
Anderson, Terry, 132, 148
Allen, Woody, 116, 122, 126, 163
Angyal, A., 148
Aristide, Jean-Bertrand, 156–57, 159, 169
Augustine, Saint, 21, 38, 169–70, 171

"Babette's Feast" (Dinesen), 5, 16, 55–57, 63. *See also* Eating
Balasuriya, Tissa, 49, 62
Barbotin, Edmond, 55, 63
Barth, Karl, 22, 38
Basil, Saint, 98, 109
Bateson, Mary Catherine, 73, 78
Beare, F. W., 148
De Beausobre, Iulia, 102–3, 109
Ben & Jerry's Homemade, Inc., 65–66, 87
Benchley, Robert, 123–24
Berger, Peter, 120, 123, 126
Bergson, Henri, 125–26
Berdayaev, Nicholas, 102, 109
Bernstein, Felicia, 96
Berrigan, Dan, 59, 63
Blanchard, Kenneth, 19, 20, 35, 37
Bly, Robert, 109
Body, the, 15, 57–58, 165. *See also* Health
Brandsma, Titus, 146
Brody, Jane, 44, 61, 62, 126

Brueggemann, Walter, xi–xii, 96, 108
Buechner, Frederick, 124, 127
Burger, Robert E., 17
Buttrick, George, 124, 127
Bynum, Caroline Walker, 52–53, 63

Cambodia, 91–92, 108
Capote, Truman, 41, 61
Carmody, John, 42, 61
Catecholamines, 121
Chariots of Fire, 30
Chittister, Joan, 3, 16, 17
"A Christmas Memory" (Capote), 41, 61
Christophers, the, 149
Clarke, Thomas, 47, 62
Coffin, William Sloane, 100, 109
Cohen, Ben, 65–66
Color Purple, The (Walker), 19, 23–24, 37, 38, 125, 160–62, 168
Commins, Gary, 125
Composing a Life (Bateson), 73, 87
Confessions, The (Augustine), 21, 38, 169–70, 171
Conway, Jil Ker, 153, 154, 167
Coomaraswamy, A. K., 88
Crossan, John Dominic, 125
Creative Suffering (De Beausobre), 102–103, 109
Crystal, Graef S., 78, 88
cummings, e. e., 13, 17

Dalai Lama, 60–61, 63
Darkness Visible (Styron), 159, 160, 168

Dark Night of the Soul, The (John of the Cross), 162–163, 168
Day, Dorothy, 47, 62
De Pree, Max, 91, 107–8, 109
Depression. *See* Persevering
Dickens, Charles, 54, 63
Dillard, Annie, 35, 39
Dinesen, Isak, 5, 16, 55–57, 63
Dostoevsky, F. M., 80–81, 88
Do What You Love and the Money Will Follow (Sinetar), 76
Downs, Thomas, 146–47, 149
Dravecky, Dave, 151–52, 159, 167

Eating, 41–63; Adam and Eve and, 44–45; and the body, 43, 57–58; as communion, 48–49, 51–53; and community, 46–48, 49, 53–55, 58; and diet, 42–43, 45; and dietary anarchy, 43–44; dysfunctional meals, 53–54; exercises, 58–61; and health, 42, 43–44; as hospitality, 46–48, 49–51, 53–55; Jesus and, 45, 46–48, 51–53, 55; marginalized and, 44, 47–48; and moderation, 51; and nutrition, 44, 58, 59, 60, 61; and obesity, 43; as occasion for disclosure, 53–57; and religion, 42–43; rituals and food, 41–42, 45, 47; and starvation, 44, 60; and the table, 47, 49, 53–55, 58; and women, 52. *See also* "Babette's Feast"
Eco, Umberto, 112, 124
Egospeak (Addeo and Burger), 6
Eliot, T. S., 5, 16
Endo, Shusaku, 101, 109
Endorphins, 121
Eucharist, 49, 51–53, 105
Exercises: eating, 58–61; excuses

not to, 169–70; forgiving, 144–47; as invitation to love, 171; laughing, 122–24; listening, 14–16; persevering, 165–67; praising, 35–37; weeping, 105–8; working, 84–87

Farrell, Edward J., 7–8
Fassel, Diane, 79, 88
Fiorenza, Francis, 67, 87
First Circle, The (Solzhenitsyn), 155
Fisher, M. F. K., 63
FitzGerald, Constance, 162, 168
Food. *See* Eating
Forgiving, 129–49; benefits of, 136, 142–44; as cancellation of a debt, 132–34; confrontation and, 134–35, 141; definition, 132–33; exercises, 144–47; and freedom, 131–32; and hate, 137, 138; and healing, 143; and new identity, 138–40; as obligation, 131; obstacles to, 140–42; as power, 138–40; and pride, 142; and repentance, 134, 141–42; to restore self-respect, 131–32; and revenge, 133–34, 135–36, 143–44; and trust, 143; as unreasonable behavior, 130–31
Fowler, Robert, 115, 125
Francis of Assisi, 21
Frank, Anne, 95, 155
Frankl, Viktor, 154
Freud, Sigmund, 125–26
Fry, William F., 121
Funk, Robert, 115–16, 125–26

Gandhi, Mohandas, 43, 62
Gaylin, Willard, 38

Gift from the Sea (Lindbergh), 4,
  16
Good Work (Schumacher), 76
Greenfield, Jeff, 65–66

Hamlet (Shakespeare), 121–22,
  126
Hammarskjold, Dag, 129, 148
Hauerwas, Stanley, 108
Haughey, John, 79, 87, 88
Havel, Václav, 115–56, 157, 167
Hawthorne, Nathaniel, 133, 148
Health, 2–3, 14, 43, 57, 79–80,
  120–22, 143
Hillesum, Etty, 95
Holiness, 118
Holy Feast, Holy Fast (Bynum),
  52–53, 63
Hope. *See* Persevering
Hospitality, 49–51, 53–55
Hugo, Victor, 138–40, 149
Humor: and Christianity, 111–14;
  definition of, 116; and freedom,
  120; and holiness, 118–20; and
  humility, 118–20. *See also*
  Laughing
Hyers, Conrad, 124

Iacocca, Lee, 6, 16
Images of Hope (Lynch), 159–60,
  161, 165, 168
Incarnation and humor, 117–18
"In Search of Our Mother's Gar-
  dens" (Walker), 74, 88

Jesus: and eating, 45, 46–48,
  51–53, 55; and forgiving, 131,
  136–37, 138, 145–46; and
  laughing, 111, 114–16; and listening, 8–9, 11–13; and persevering, 163; and praising; 21,

35; and weeping, 99–102, 103,
  104–5; and work, 69–70;
John of the Cross, Saint, 162, 163,
  168
John XXIII, Pope, 124, 127
John Paul II, Pope, 81, 88
Johnson, Samuel, 21
Johnson, Spencer, 19, 20, 35, 37
Johnson, James Weldon, 68–69, 87
Jokes, 111. *See also* Humor;
  Laughing

Kapleau, Philip, 1, 16
Khmer Rouge, 91–92
Kierkegaard, Søren, 117–18, 125
King, Martin Luther, Jr., 137–138,
  142, 148, 149
Klassen, William, 148
Kugelman, Richard, 148
Kundera, Milan, 111, 123, 124,
  126
Kushi, Michio, 62

Laborem Exercens, 81
Lapsley, James, 148
Laughing (sense of humor),
  111–27; benefits of, 120–22;
  definition of, 116; exercises,
  122–24; and freedom, 118–20;
  Gospels and humor, 114, 115,
  124; and holiness, 118; and
  honesty, 118–19; and the Incarnation, 117–18; and incongruity, 112–13, 116–18; Jesus
  and humor, 111, 114–15; and
  medicine, 120–22; obstacles to
  alliance between religion and
  humor, 112–14; and pain,
  119–20, 123; and parables, 119;
  and physical health, 120–22. *See
  also* Humor

Leucke, Richard, 89
Les Miserables (Hugo), 138–40, 149
Lewis, C. S., 20, 22, 23, 31, 34, 38, 52, 62, 125, 152, 167
Lightner, Candy, 147, 149
Lindbergh, Anne Morrow, 4, 16
Lindquist, Ray, 108
Listening, 1–16; as active, not passive, 2, 3, 14–16; benefits of, 13–14; and blood pressure reduction, 2–3; difference between hearing and, 3; as discovery of self, 5–6, 9; exercises, 14–16; as healing, 2–3, 12–13; instead of speaking, 10–11; and physical benefits, 2–3, 14; qualities of good, 7–10; rarity of, 6–7; reflected in body language, 12, 14; to silence, 4–6; and solitude, 4; and truth, 3–4; use of parables in, 12–13
Listeners: Jesus as listener, 8–9, 11–13; qualities of, 7–10
Lombardi, Vince, 28, 38
Lowell, James Russell, 50, 62
Lynch, James, 2–3, 16
Lynch, William, 159–60, 161, 165, 168

Mandela, Nelson, 154, 159
Markings (Hammarskjöld), 129, 148
Mary, mother of Jesus, 21
Meals. *See* Eating
Merton, Thomas, 33, 38, 119, 120, 126
Moody, Raymond A., 120–21, 126
Moule, C. D. F., 148
Moynahan, Michael, 125

Name of the Rose, The (Eco), 112, 124
Niebuhr, Reinhold, 113, 116, 125
Nightclub Years, The (Allen), 116
No Longer Enemies, Not Yet Friends (Downs), 146–47
Nouwen, Henri, 50, 62

Olsen, Tillie, 5, 16
O'Neill, June, 73, 87
One Day in the Life of Ivan Denisovich (Solzhenitsyn), 154–55
One-Minute Manager, The (Blanchard and Johnson), 19, 20, 35, 37

Parks, Sharon, 63
Patience. *See* Persevering
Paul, Apostle, 7, 49, 70, 133, 159, 164
Paul Bunyan (Stevens) 59–60
Persevering, 151–68: benefits of, 154; and "dark night," 161–64; and depression, 157–59, 164–65; exercises, 165–67; and flexibility, 152–53; and friendship, 161; and God, 161–64, 167; honesty, humility, and, 152; and hope, 159–60, 161, 166; obstacles to, 164–65; optimism, 165–67; and patience, 161, 166; and resiliency, 153–54; of the saints, 164; symbols of, 152, 155–57; and survival, 153–55
Pilgrim at Tinker Creek (Dillard), 35, 39
Pinter, Harold, 5, 16
Plato, 88
Post, Emily, 47, 62

Post, Gregory, 62
Praising, 19–39; and awkwardness, 26–27; benefits of, 34–35; difference between thanking and, 24–26; and emotions, 32–34; exercises, 35–37; faith as, 21; and God, 20, 22–24, 31, 35, 36–37; and hubris, 29–30; and jealousy, 29; obstacles to, 26–34; prayer as, 22–23; prayer life and, 35, 36; and pride, 29–31; reasons people do not praise, 26–34; and schoolchildren statistics, 27, 38; self-centeredness as impediment to, 31–32; and surprise, 23–24; thanks and, 24–26; as truth-telling, 21–22
Praiser(s): Jesus as, 21, 35; qualities of, 34–35
Praise Singer, The (Renault), 39

Ratushinskaya, Irina, 154
Renault, Mary, 39
Road from Coorain, The (Ker Conway), 153, 154
Roetzel, C. J., 148
Rohrlick, Jay, 79, 88
Romero, Oscar, 79, 98
Rule of St. Benedict, 80–81

Sakharov, Andrei, 154
Scarlet Letter, The (Hawthorne), 133, 148
Schaef, Anne Wilson, 88
Schumacher, E. F., 75, 76, 87
Schweitzer, Albert, 170
Seton, Elizabeth Bayley (Mother Seton), 157–58, 159, 168
Shakespeare, William, 121–22, 126

Shea, John, 33–34, 39
Sider, Ron, 62
Silence, 4–6, 15
Silence (Endo), 101, 109
Silences (Olsen), 5, 16
Sinetar, Marsha, 76–77, 88
Smith, Adam, 73, 87
Soelle, Dorothee, 80, 88, 94, 108
Solitude, 4
Solzhenitsyn, Alexander, 154–55, 156, 167
Steere, Douglas, 17, 89
Stevens, James, 59–60
Styron, William, 159, 160, 168
Suffering. *See* Weeping
Suffering Presence: Theological Reflections on Medicine, the Mentally Handicapped, and the Church (Hauerwas), 108

Take the Money and Run (Allen), 116
Tears. *See* Weeping
Teilhard de Chardin, Pierre, 75–76, 88
Ten Boom, Corrie, 95
Terkel, Studs, 75, 86, 87, 89
Trocmé, Andre, 95
Turner, Charles, 62
Twain, Mark, 121, 126, 169

Vanier, Jean, 96, 108
Via, Dan O., 125
Vietnam, 146–47
Volf, Miroslav, 71
Vonnegut, Kurt, 82, 89

Walker, Alice, 19, 23–24, 37, 38, 74, 88, 160–62, 168
Wallenburg, Raoul, 95

Walsh, Kevin, 86, 89
Wealth of Nations (Smith), 73, 87
Weeping, 91–109; as beginning of
    self-discovery, 95; benefits of,
    104–5; and common humanity,
    92, 94–95, 97–98, 106–7; and
    community, 94–95, 98; and
    complaining, 96–97; and con-
    flict, 97–98; as countercultural,
    94, 104; characteristics of those
    who weep, 97–99; to exercise,
    105–8; God, 96, 99–102; and
    the Holocaust, 92, 95–96; and
    hope, 99; and pain, painlessness,
    93–94; and serenity, 103; and
    social stigma, 92–93; and suffer-
    ing with another, 92, 93,
    94–95, 97–98, 99–102, 103,
    104–5
Wesley, John, 42
Westermann, Claus, 21, 25, 38
Wicks, Robert, 3, 16, 17
Wiesel, Elie, 100, 109
Williams, Paul, 8, 17
Working, 65–89; alienation around,
    80–81, 83; as benefitting the
    worker, 75–76; and the body,
    66, 75; and compensation, 78;
    and contemplation, 84, 86–87;

and creativity, 66, 73, 74, 75;
    definition of, 71–72, 74; and di-
    versity, 82–83, 85; exercises,
    84–87; faith and, 70; and fulfill-
    ment, 82, 85; and gender issues,
    71–73; and God, 67–69;
    "good," 76–78; healthy, 79–80;
    impersonal, 78–79; in the home,
    71–72; Jesus and, 69–70; and
    justice, 73, 78; and liturgy, 84;
    and meaning, 74, 76–78; mis-
    sion qualities of, 69–70, 86; and
    money, 76; as partnership with
    God, 67, 69–70; and product,
    72–73; and quality, 83, 85–86;
    and social mission, 65–66;
    "soul," 74–75; soulless, 75–76;
    valuing, 81–83; and wages, 71,
    73, 88; and women, 72, 73,
    82–83, 88; and workaholism,
    78–80
Working (Terkel), 75, 86
*Work in the Spirit: Toward a Theol-
    ogy of Work* (Volf), 71

Wuellner, Flora Slosson, 15, 17

Xerox Corporation, 82–83, 89